TRIVIUM MASTERY: THE INTERSECTION OF THREE ROADS

How to Give Your Child an Authentic Classical Home Education

Diane B. Lockman

Outskirts Press, Inc.
Denver, Colorado

Trivium Mastery: The Intersection of Three Roads
How to Give Your Child an Authentic Classical Home Education
All Rights Reserved.
Copyright © 2009 Diane B. Lockman
The Classical Scholar (http://classicalscholar.com)
v6.0

Cover Design by Vincent Franco of freshivore (http://www.freshivore.net)

Outskirts Press, Inc.
http://www.outskirtspress.com

ISBN: 978-1-4327-3328-5

Library of Congress Control Number: 2008940342

Outskirts Press and the "OP" logo are trademarks belonging to Outskirts Press, Inc.

PRINTED IN THE UNITED STATES OF AMERICA

For my beloved family:
David, Meredith, and Connor

&

"For freedom Christ has set us free.
Stand firm, therefore, and do not submit again to a yoke of slavery."
Galatians 5:1 (NRSV)

Contents

Preface

PART ONE: A MISSING INHERITANCE

The First Road: Language

The Second Road: Thought

The Third Road: Speech

The Destination: Mastery

PART TWO: TWELVE CLASSICAL MAKEOVERS

First Family: John, Rebecca, Two Sons, and Two Daughters

Second Family: Joe, Anne, Three Sons, and Two Daughters

Third Family: David, Ruth, and Eleven Children

Fourth Family: Henry, Jean, and Twin Sons

Fifth Family: Mark, Julia, One Son, and One Daughter

Appendices: Assessment Tools

Preface

Call me responsible. Call me curious. Call me thorough. You see, my prior training as a CPA prepared me for this new adventure. After all those years of chasing down details to discover the truth, I am pretty good at sifting through information and deciding what is relevant and what is irrelevant. I've had lots of practice at summarizing evidence and developing clear, practical action steps for my partners and clients.

So, in hindsight, this latest adventure doesn't really surprise me. When I first began my journey towards an authentic classical Christian home education, I naively embraced the current teaching of the leading renewal movement. Although I'm generally not a "glass half empty" kind of person, I did learn as an auditor that the truth is not often immediately revealed. Time, persistent questions, and research eventually yield results that usually look more accurate than a first glance at the data.

Consequently, when I began to struggle with the layers and layers of rigorous academic requirements of the "new" classical method, I decided to do a little research about the history of classical education. I wanted to know what a classical education really looked like. Did ancient Greeks and Romans do all that the modern renewal movement wanted me to do? How did the early Christians tweak the model to make it their own? When was the classical model replaced in our country's educational paradigm? Was the current home schooling model true to the past?

During this research, I began to feel an unusual mixture of rising empowerment and indignation. The classical Christian education that was my rightful inheritance had been taken from me by educational bureaucrats. Generations of well-meaning parents and innocent children never received their intended bequest. Instead, the "new" classical method being popularized in the home schooling community looked more like the public school paradigm than the original classical model. In my research, I discovered that the primary premise upon which the "new" classical method was based had no evidentiary support other than one woman's personal experience. Speculation and hearsay fueled the rumor that soon became an urban legend. Armed with a new perspective, I decided that I wanted to reclaim our classical inheritance, but one major question loomed in my mind. How could it be done?

Tweak. Tweak. Tweak. My home became a laboratory, and my children were the guinea pigs. In the midst of all the tweaking, I began to see that a true classical Christian education could be simply reduced to the acquisition of three major skills (language, thought, and speech), and that when those skills were substantially mastered, the kids would have the tools necessary to delve deeply into serious content like the adult classics and higher level sciences. Once I boiled it down to the essentials, the task no longer seemed so overwhelming. Fleshing it out in practice became an open vista of personal choices that mirrored our kids' learning styles, passions, and abilities. Liberated from the urban legend, we were able to experience the freedom of a true classical Christian education.

Exposition of errors, no matter how innocent or unintentional, is not enough. I learned as an auditor to report such aberrations to leaders who could adjust the course of action and ensure corrective measures. Therein is the genesis of this book. You see, I just couldn't sit on the truth about classical education and participate in the cover up. I am compelled to share the results of my open lab in the hope that you can confirm my findings. Let's start an ongoing dialogue about the pragmatic application of a true classical model at home and recover our inheritance together.

May you raise your own classical scholars in wisdom and truth.

Diane B. Lockman
Indianapolis, Indiana
October 2008

PART ONE

&

A MISSING INHERITANCE

Chapter 2
The Millennial Foundation

Classical education, born in ancient Greece, flourished for nearly a thousand years in the West until the collapse of the Roman Empire in the fifth century A.D. Come with me for a quick overview of the millennial foundation of classical education.

An Enlightened, Mature Mind

Paideia ("pie-DAY-uh"), the Greek word for instruction or discipline, referred to the process of forming an enlightened, mature mind. Unlike many of today's educational institutions, the paideia was not concerned with vocational training, quality control, or meeting objective standards. Rather, learning was the path to a higher nature through the exploration of abstract concepts such as liberty, beauty, justice, and courage with the expectation that such examination would lead to noble character and gracious behavior. These transformed few would enrich society.

The paideia of a Greek child began with reading and writing. Although every student had a writing tablet, the spoken word took precedence over the written word. Literature was written to be read aloud. Entire passages of *The Iliad* and *The Odyssey*, epic poems by Homer, were committed to memory for later recital.

Having learned basic reading and writing, Greek children then improved those two skills within the context of classic literature. Classic literature was selected for study (usually Homer, Euripides, Menander, or Demosthenes), and the student copied the text in Attic Greek. Next, the text was read aloud with particular attention to effective delivery of meaning and meter. Then the text was translated from Attic Greek to Koine Greek (the spoken language), and certain passages were committed to memory. Finally, the moral of the passage was evaluated. Once the classic was thoroughly read and understood, three written paraphrases were composed: strict, freer, and original.

Aspiring young leaders continued their education for another two years; participation in higher education certified full social and political status. The elite gathered for athletics at the gymnasium then dismissed to study rhetoric, philosophy, medicine, or law. Every leader was expected to publicly discuss any subject with skill, so training in rhetoric was rigorous. Once the extensive rules of rhetoric were mastered, young men analyzed model passages of famous orators and practiced writing their own versions. Eventually, they were equipped to write their own speeches with style.

As for philosophy, a young man joined a "school" like Plato's Academy or Aristotle's Lyceum, studied the history of philosophy beginning with Thales, and examined the particular school's writings in detail. Wandering philosophers or private teachers held lectures outside of class.

The philosopher Socrates, revealed in the pages of Plato's writings, was the most famous educator of ancient Greece. He employed a form of inquiry known as Socratic Dialogue in the paideia of his students. In its purest form, Socratic dialogue is a series of leading questions posed by the teacher or tutor that assist the student in self-discovery and understanding. Aristotle, a student of Plato, employed Socratic Dialogue and empirical observation in the paideia of his renowned student Alexander the Great.

The Seven Liberal Arts of Free Men

Adopting the Greek idea of paideia, the Romans created a system of study known as the "seven liberal arts" which was intended to provide general knowledge and intellectual skills to the leaders of society. The English word liberal derives from the Latin adjective liberalis which means "freeborn condition" thus explaining why these arts were taught to free men (the elite) while the lower classes were taught the servile arts (derived from the Latin word, servus, meaning "servant"). Not surprisingly, the servile arts were occupational in nature.

The seven liberal arts were divided into two phases: the trivium (intersection of three roads) and the quadrivium (four roads). Young patricians pursued the first level of learning, the trivium, which included simultaneous acquisition of three skills: grammar, logic, and rhetoric. Once these three skills were substantially mastered, students studied arithmetic, geometry, astronomy, and music theory which together comprise the more difficult mathematically oriented quadrivium. Those Romans who wished to pursue further education attended colleges, communities of apprentices, led by a master.

Young Romans followed Greek methods for learning how to read, write, and deliver orations. In addition to translating the Greek classics, Roman children memorized the Latin writings of Virgil, Terence, Cicero, and Horace. The speeches of Cicero, Livy, Cato, and the Gracchi were studied and imitated. Buildings were not dedicated for education; rather, a few pupils gathered around a learned man in the courtyard.

During Jesus' life, the Roman Empire occupied Palestine, and the influence of the Greco-Roman concept of education was so pervasive that some rabbis worried that their Jewish heritage would be obliterated. Their concerns were misplaced, however, as the skills of the classical trivium were adopted by Jews to translate, study, memorize, and recite the classic text, the Torah. Interestingly, anyone familiar with the classical trivium will recognize a fellow rhetorician in the Apostle Paul as his letters are full of classical rhetorical devices. Christian leaders in the late Roman Empire, particularly clergy, were regularly trained in the classical model.

* * * * *

When the Roman Empire collapsed in the 5th century A.D., the ancient paideia was generally forgotten. More important matters of survival and societal reorganization took precedence over education. Literacy plummeted, and the millennial foundation of classical education lay dormant for nearly four hundred years.

Chapter 3
Christianizing Classical Education

During the 9th Century A.D., the classical education of the ancients experienced an apparent rebirth when Charlemagne was crowned the first Holy Roman Emperor. What had appeared dead for nearly four hundred years had actually been kept alive by a small but dedicated group of monks, priests, and bishops. Although the widespread access of classical education had been significantly reduced, the second thousand years witnessed a beautiful transformation as Christian classics were incorporated into the corpus of the classical approach, and access was once made again available to the general population.

Perfecting Christian Leaders

Appalled by the fact that only ecclesiastics could read, Emperor Charlemagne established the "Palace School" for himself, his family, and young noblemen. The skills of the trivium and the subjects of the quadrivium were both taught. Believing that the ancient classical education could not serve its true purpose unless integrated with Christian teaching and writing, Charlemagne also required study of the *Old* and *New Testaments*, writings of the early Church fathers, liturgical books, biographies of the saints, and canon law along with the ancient Greek and Roman texts.

Like the Greeks, Romans, and Jews before them, these students translated source documents from the original language to their vernacular language. Young men of this period learned Greek and Latin for the purpose of reading the original texts. A Koine Greek translation of the *Old Testament*, created in Alexandria during the 3rd to 1st centuries B.C., allowed Palace School scholars to bypass Hebrew if they wanted since they could read the entire Scriptures in Greek.

Some monastic orders emulated the Palace School and opened monastic schools throughout the realm. These schools enabled many members of the peasant class to become literate. Thus, Charlemagne ignited the spread of classical Christian education beyond the palace, though his goal was only to perfect leaders through the study of Greek, Roman, and Christian thinkers under the guidance of the Holy Spirit.

Confederations of Higher Learning

Universities, or loose confederations of teachers, evolved from the royal and ecclesiastical schools during the late 11th and 12th centuries A.D. Initially without campuses, classes were taught in homes and churches.

Students joined the universitas ("the community") at fourteen or fifteen years of age and began learning the three skills of the trivium. When the trivium was substantially mastered, the Bachelor of Arts Degree was earned, and work on the quadrivium began. Upon mastery of the quadrivium, the Masters of Arts Degree was awarded. Courses were centered about great writers and their books, not subjects. No electives were permitted, and mastery of the seven liberal arts usually took at least six years.

Around 1300 A.D., three new areas of study were offered: theology (the study of God), law (the study of human society), and medicine (the study of material order). Acquiring a Doctorate degree in one of these areas could take up to thirteen more years. Theology was both the most prestigious and difficult area of study. The Universities of Bologna (Italy), Paris (France), and Oxford (England) were among the first official schools of higher learning in Europe. Financial funding for the first universities was provided by individual families or, in the case of Paris University, by the Roman Catholic Church.

* * * * *

In examining the effects of the first revival of classical education, the phrase "beauty from ashes" comes to mind. According to an ancient myth, a breathtaking bird called the phoenix erupts in flames and turns to cold, gray ashes only to experience a rebirth more gorgeous than before. In God's sovereign timing, the Roman Empire collapsed after Christianity had experienced wild growth. Faithful monks preserved the methods and documents of the classical tradition while Charlemagne infused new life into the tradition with Christian classics and study of Scripture. Finally, the pinnacle of education near the end of the second thousand years of classical education was the study of theology. The mainstream pagan education had been redeemed by Christian content.

Chapter 4
The Death Knell Threatens

You cannot write a conclusion until the story is over. A variation of the original classical Christian education of the second millennium still shudders with life and occasionally threatens to become a full-blown movement of the Holy Spirit. Follow the path of classical Christian education to the shores of North America, and discover when your inheritance was buried and how a small group of home schooling pioneers have reshaped the common school model into a new or "neoclassical" approach.

Schools Take Shape

New England Puritans valued education for religious reasons. Typical fathers read the translated Bible to their children daily. As the economy prospered, servants and apprentices migrated to New England. Most of these immigrants were not originally Puritan, and concern grew that these people would be poor citizens. In 1642, a Massachusetts law was passed requiring the head of the household to provide instruction in reading, religion, and civil law to their charges (children, servants, and apprentices). This act burdened household instruction as more than a family reading of the Bible was required.

By 1647, the Commonwealth of Massachusetts mandated every community with 50 households to hire a teacher of reading and writing, and communities with 150 households were obligated to open a grammar school which taught basic reading, writing, and arithmetic. Christian ministers were usually hired as schoolmasters.

Concerned with training Puritan leaders, the first college preparatory secondary school was opened in 1635 in Boston, Massachusetts to prepare young men for Harvard College which was opened the following year. Designed for Puritan sons who were destined for leadership positions in church and state, the classical Christian curriculum of Boston Latin School was augmented with key writings of the Protestant Reformation.

Ancient Greek and Latin classics were read in the original language; the Harvard entrance exam required an understanding of both languages.

Extensive knowledge of western history and literature was acquired. Additionally, advanced arithmetic and specialized occupational training in the areas of surveying and navigation were taught.

Similar elite schools opened in New York and Charleston. Schools in the Southern colonies were rare due to the rural dispersion of population, so young men of social status were initially home educated then privately tutored in ancient languages and classic literature. Some young men were sent to England and Scotland for further education.

Affluent young ladies were often sent to finishing schools where they learned handwriting, French, music, dance, and needlework. Youths unable to afford secondary schools or employ private tutors found apprenticeships where they learned a trade.

Initially, classical Christian education flourished in America's first colleges. Harvard, the first undergraduate institution in North America, was established to educate Puritan ministers. By 1755, there were seven colleges in North America each of which used the classical model: the College of William and Mary, St. John's College, Yale, Princeton, Columbia, and The University of Pennsylvania. Ancient languages, ancient history, theology, and mathematics were the primary focus; astronomy, physics, modern history, and politics were added later.

Upon graduation, most men became Protestant clergy or pursued a law practice. Of humorous note, the fifty-six signers of the Declaration of Independence tended toward a law career: twenty-eight were lawyers, ten were merchants, five were doctors, five were government appointees, four were farmers, three were ministers, and one was a surveyor. Over sixty percent of the signers had been classically educated, either abroad or in one of the seven colleges mentioned above.

Nurseries for Free Men

As the immigrant population increased to 2.5 million during the mid-1800s, a group of educational reformers in New England began to advocate for tuition-free "common schools" and compulsory attendance. Class differences preoccupied thought even though Americans had rejected monarchy and a system of landed aristocracy.

Advocates maintained that a common system of education was necessary in a democracy. All citizens, with certain blatant exceptions, needed an equal chance to advance by their skills and hard work. Common schools, touted as the key institution for educating citizens, were popularly called 'nurseries for free men.'

Education reformers had other concerns including idle, vagrant youth in urban cities, and different political (monarchy) and religious (Roman Catholic) views which needed to be tempered with "American" (Protestant) values. At first, Protestants argued over which denomination would prevail in doctrinal content but eventually agreed to teach non-sectarian values such as hard work, morals, and civic obligations.

Already a leader in education, Massachusetts commenced the march to educate all Americans in 1852 when it passed the first compulsory school law. Although there were pockets of resistance nationwide, such opposition was generally localized, and by 1918, every state in the union had ratified compulsion.

College or Vocation?

During the early stages of American public education, a philosophical debate arose as to whether secondary education should prepare the student for college or vocation. In 1892, a committee of the National Council of Education issued a comprehensive report with the following recommendations for all U. S. public schools: 12 years of total study (six years elementary, three years junior, and three years senior) and four curricula tracks based upon language study. The first track, the Classical Programme, included four years of Latin and three years of Greek. College-bound track number two, the Latin-Scientific Programme, included four years of Latin and one year each of Trigonometry and Advanced Algebra.

The two tracks for the vocation-bound student included the English track and the Modern Language track. All four tracks resembled a classical Christian education in that western literature, composition, and Greco-Roman, French, English, and American histories were taught. Were it not for two obstacles, a secularized version of a classical education might still exist in the American public school system.

The Funeral Dirge Commences

One obstacle to the full application of the National Council recommendation was a lack of qualified teachers. The supply of

12

classically-trained teachers could not meet the demand, and those teachers who were currently employed by the schools would require extensive training to equip them for this level of rigor. More significantly, there remained a powerful group of educators who did not agree that American public high schools should be college-preparatory institutions.

By 1918, these educators won the debate as evidenced in U. S. Department of the Interior, Bureau of Education, bulletin no. 35, which outlined the main priorities of public high schools in the *Cardinal Principles of Secondary Education:*

1. Health
2. Command of fundamental processes
3. Worthy home membership
4. Vocation
5. Civic education
6. Worthy use of leisure
7. Ethical character

Health and physical education classes, home economics classes, machine shop classes, and extracurricular clubs were established in response to this pronouncement. Most striking is the absence of academic focus; reading, writing, and arithmetic were considered the "fundamental processes" necessary for life. History was replaced with Social Studies. According to the bulletin:

> "Education in the United States should be guided by a clear conception of democracy. The purpose of democracy is to so organize society so that each member may develop his personality primarily through activities designed for the well-being of his fellow members and of society as a whole. Democracy must place chief reliance upon education. Consequently, education in a democracy, both within and without the school, should develop in each individual the knowledge, interests, ideals, habits, and powers whereby he will find his place and use that place to shape both himself and society toward ever nobler ends."

Wrestling with the writings of great thinkers was no longer an achievable goal. Instead, a mere grasp of the most rudimentary abilities would suffice, and those abilities would be exercised in learning one's servile role in society. In 1892, an institutionalized version of classical education was the goal for all American students. A scant twenty-six years later, a powerful group of educators issued the seven *Cardinal Principles* which effectively removed classical education, both secular and Christian, from the American public system. This approach that had successfully trained national leaders on two continents for over two thousand years was replaced with pragmatic aptitude training that prepares the student to function in the economy.

The Contemporary Disaster

Today, the curriculum in American public schools bears no resemblance to Charlemagne's redeemed classical education. The classics of Western Civilization, Socratic dialogue, world history, and Christian texts are nowhere to be found in this example from the Revised Code of Washington State, Law 28A, regarding public school curriculum:

> "All common schools shall give instruction in reading, penmanship, orthography, written and mental arithmetic, geography, U.S. history, English grammar, physiology and hygiene with special reference to the effects of alcohol and drug abuse on the human system, science with special reference to the environment and such other studies as may be prescribed by rule of the superintendent of public instruction. All teachers shall stress the importance of cultivation of manners, the fundamental principles of honesty, industry and economy, the minimum requisites for good health including the beneficial effect of physical exercise and methods to prevent exposure to and transmission of sexually-transmitted diseases, and the worth of kindness to all living creatures and the land. The prevention of child abuse may be offered as part of the curriculum in the common schools."

Non-sectarian values of manners, honesty, industry, and economy are similar to those outlined 150 years earlier in the beginnings of the common school movement. Consistent with the 1918 *Cardinal Principles*, health issues still color the curriculum. Lectures, textbooks, and tests have replaced reading, writing, and speaking about the classics. Memorization and recitation are defunct. Discussion of abstract concepts, as relevant today as they were 3,000 years ago, has been replaced with discussion of tolerance and moral relativism.

14

According to the *Encyclopedia Britannica*, "formal education has assumed many of the responsibilities formerly reserved for family, religion, and social organizations. Most Americans expect schools to provide children with skills, values, and behaviors that will help them become responsible citizens, contribute to social stability in the country, and increase American economic productivity."

Based upon the business concept of Total Quality Management, the most recent trend in public education is Outcome-Based Education (OBE) which attempts to measure student performance against objective standards. The recently enacted federal law called "No Child Left Behind" is an example of outcome-based education. Characteristics of OBE include standardized tests, pass/fail status instead of letter grades, and replacement of facts with feelings. Some educators consider the current trend as a dumbing down of America. Certainly, the underlying philosophy that children are manufactured components machined to an acceptable quality standard for incorporation in the country's economic engine is antithetical to the classical Christian educational model. One of the many risks of such an approach is that forty-nine million students will learn "what to think" and not "how to think." The prospects for reversal of this trend appear dim.

Ah, but hope does not disappoint. Just like the perfect timing of Charlemagne's reforms in 800 A.D., classical education may be on the verge of a second revival within a tiny, obscure segment of the general population called Christian home schooling.

Chapter 5
The Neoclassical Urban Legend

With the exception of a few private academies, a classical curriculum was effectively removed from American schools in 1918 when the U. S. Bureau of Education required the implementation of the seven cardinal principles in every high school. For nearly 75 years, classical methods and classical content were absent from American primary and secondary education. Lost. Missing. Dead. Or so it would seem.

Although Christians believe history is linear, it often appears to repeat in cycles, and just like the dark period of the early middle ages when it appeared that classical education was dead, a movement to resurrect an old model was underway. In the last decade of the 20th century, God in His sovereignty began to stir some pivotal Christians to explore Western Civilization's past and reintroduce classical ideas. Praise God for this handful of Christian educators! Like Emperor Charlemagne, they were faithful in introducing believers to a classical Christian education. A renewal movement was born within the Christian home schooling community that continues to spread as more and more people hear about the benefits of a classical education.

However grateful I am for their obedience, though, I see this revival as a relay race where one runner begins the race and hands the baton off to another runner. In their good faith efforts and initial zeal to persuade others to adopt a classical education, I believe they have based their reconstruction of classical education on a faulty premise. Herein lies the crux of my argument. As a collective body, we have started the race well, but we need to make a few corrections to the course. Let me explain.

The Faulty Premise

During the 1940s, British author Dorothy Sayers presented an essay at Oxford University called *The Lost Tools of Learning* in which she compared the sorry state of modern education with the historically preferable state of classical education. She proposed that we had lost the tools necessary for learning how to think. Though unappreciated at the time it was presented, Sayers' essay kindled the fire that began the contemporary home schooling renewal movement almost fifty years later.

Early in the essay, Sayers accurately recounts the composition of the medieval classical education: first, the trivium which included the "tools" of learning: grammar (language acquisition), logic (critical thinking), and rhetoric (written and oral composition), which young men tackled before moving on to the quadrivium (arithmetic, astronomy, music, and geometry.) In her anguish over the modern state of nations where men and women don't know how to think, Sayers speculated that there may be a connection between the medieval trivium and the stages of child development. She posited:

> "What if the psychology of the child progresses through the three stages of the trivium?"

Sayers names the three stages of child development poll-parrot, pert, and poetic; she then concludes that the three skills of the trivium are "singularly appropriate" to the three stages of child development. Based upon Sayers' recounting of her own personal experience as a child, preteen, and teen, this hypothesis seems to make sense. Unfortunately, her hypothesis has never been clinically proven and no evidence has been gathered as proof, other than her testimony of her own mental development. In fact, Sayers absolves herself from blame by saying, "My views about child psychology are, I admit, neither orthodox nor enlightened."

Put this in perspective. Imagine that your teen is performing a scientific experiment. She develops her hypothesis and constructs an experiment to test the hypothesis. If she merely relies upon her expected results, would you allow her to conclude that her hypothesis is valid? Of course not! You would teach her to conduct the experiment, record actual results, and use them to evaluate the hypothesis. Why then, would the home schooling community so eagerly embrace Sayers' untested theory of child mental development as the foundation for the urban legend of the 12 year, three stage trivium? Simply put, no good reason exists.

A Masquerade

As I mentioned previously, I am grateful for those heroes who reintroduced classical education to the home schooling community. The methods and content of classical Christian education constitute an incredibly rich inheritance that I wish all home school students would enjoy. However, my objections relate to the current classical renewal movement's uncritical affirmation of Sayers' personal opinion on child

17

development as gospel truth and unquestioning application of Sayers' hypothesis to a 12 year public school schedule.

In practice, this new or "neoclassical" approach takes the public school model of 1892 (12 years of subjects) and divides it into three, four year stages (grades 1-4 "grammar"; grades 5-8 "logic"; grades 9-12 "rhetoric"). No wonder families who adopt this model throw up their hands in frustration! If you look closely, this is a public school paradigm imposed upon classical education content. Tacking on subjects such as classic literature, ancient languages, formal logic, and oratory doesn't make an education classical.

Concurrent ≠ Consecutive

Sayers clearly states that she is not trained in child psychology. Neither she nor later scientists ever performed clinical trials to prove or disprove her hypothesis. In all my reading, I have not found any proof, other than Sayers' own experience, that children follow three stages of development that correlate to a three stage trivium. Moreover, the new classical curriculum developed entirely without reference to any theory of child mental development. Even if there were three stages of child development they could not correlate because there are no stages in the historical trivium!

Earlier, I defined the Latin word trivium as the "intersection of three roads." The mental picture implies that all three roads are capable of simultaneous, intermittent travel quite unlike the linear idea of a chronological path where you complete one stage before moving on to future stages. To visualize the classical trivium, imagine a three dimensional cube with x, y, and z planes. Practically, a person can work on all three skills at once. The central point at which the three roads of the trivium intersect represents mastery of the skills (language, thought, and speech), and it is at this intersection that the apprentice has the necessary tools to move on to deeper study of knowledge within specific disciplines. Therefore, a true classical education involves concurrent mastery of the three skills as opposed to consecutive mastery of three stages.

An Artificially Imposed Criterion

What is so sacred about a twelve year schedule? Learning happens throughout life. Realistically, attentive parents begin to teach the three skills of the classical trivium from birth without ever writing a lesson plan.

We instinctively know that we need to bring our precious infants into the world of language, thought, and communication simultaneously.

Remember that the twelve year educational paradigm originated in 1892 as a response to the growing immigrant explosion. The idea was to divide and to conquer. The academic year was divided into segments, the school day was divided into periods, and the topics were divided into subjects. How much more manageable the growing population was when you could corral them into buildings and teach them what to think. You know where this educational paradigm leads.

Classical scholars did not impose a twelve year trivium on their apprentices. Grade levels were nonexistent. Apprentices joined masters rather late in childhood (between the ages of eleven and fourteen) at which point they quickly mastered the three skills of grammar, logic, and rhetoric. Once having perfected these skills, they were able to study discrete ideas in depth. For them, the body of knowledge was limited to a few disciplines; for our teens, the possibilities for in-depth exploration of ideas are virtually limitless. If we desire to have our children master a classical education, why would we rely on a methodology for a pedestrian education?

* * * * *

Legends are stories that have been handed down over generations to explain events or traditions without an objective basis. The urban legend of the "twelve-year, three-stage trivium" is a commonly held story used to legitimize the imposition of a public school schedule on a classical education. Over the past two decades, countless home school parents have unquestioningly embraced the urban legend as truth; consequently, they have labored under a false premise that obscures the rich beauty of a real classical education, namely, true foundational skills are developed in concert with one another. A sequential approach fails to satisfy.

Soon, the next generation of home school students educated under this neoclassical approach will begin to home educate their own children. We must recognize that this approach, masquerading as classical, enslaves us to a public school approach taught in a different environment. We need to stop pretending to be public school teachers with our neat little workbooks and meaningless tasks. A real classical education is much easier to execute and frees the family to pursue the richness of their Western inheritance in ways that uniquely fit the abilities, interests, and gifts of the child.

Chapter 6
Three Roads to Recovery

Getting back to the basics of your classical inheritance is so much easier than you may think. If you have been operating under the neoclassical model for any length of time, you will probably find the freedom of a real classical Christian education exhilarating. Freed of the structure of the twelve-year, three-stage urban legend, you can relax and enjoy your children as you teach three simple skills: language, thought, and speech.

Where are you going?

If you recall, the ancient definition of the classical trivium is the intersection of three roads. Each of the three skills represents a road. Each of the roads culminates in a point which I will call "substantial mastery." Over the years, you will teach your child each of the three skills, performing periodic evaluations to assess mastery. This process will take years, but depending on when you start and how your child progresses, you will eventually reach the intersection of substantial mastery.

When you finally arrive at the intersection, your role as parent shifts from that of teacher to guide. The child who has substantially mastered the three skills of the trivium has all the necessary tools to study any discipline in depth. Note that substantial mastery is not the same as perfection. Naturally, few people ever achieve absolute mastery over the three skills, so as you expose your teens to the inherited body of Western knowledge during the high school years, you might also continue to teach some final advanced skills of the trivium like how to develop a thesis and defend a dissertation.

To summarize the big picture, the first several years of classical home schooling should be devoted to developing the skills that will allow your teenager to interpret meaning. Authentic classical education has always been primarily interested in "ideas," so your first task is to give them the tools for learning, and your second task is to supervise the discussion and interpretation of ideas.

How will you get there?

Start with your own education. In order to "teach to mastery," you need to be familiar with the foundational building blocks of the English language, critical thinking (especially arithmetic), and both oral and written communication. Look over my road maps for mastery, and assess your own level of knowledge. If there are areas that are weak, plan to shore up this knowledge before you need to teach it. You know most of this basic information, but you may need to refresh your memory in some areas.

Next, take a few days off, answer the interview questions (appendix) and make time to assess each child using the three road maps for mastery. Use the Assessment Tools (appendix), or establish your own criteria for determining whether they have mastered a skill or not. Once you know where each child stands, prepare a simple short-term plan for each child like the ones in Part Two: Twelve Classical Makeovers.

When should you start?

Realistically, involved parents unknowingly teach all three skills from an early age as a matter of daily life in the family. The new parent who enthusiastically gathers the small toddler into her lap for a snuggle and a good board book is already teaching language. The playful parent who regularly works puzzles and plays games with the child is teaching critical thinking skills, and the parent who consistently includes the children in adult conversations teaches effective oral communication. Look for real-life teaching opportunities in every circumstance.

How long will it take?

That depends on each child, too. In our family, our kids had mastered language and thinking skills before they mastered oral and written communication skills, so when your teen is regularly writing analytical short essays, he or she is ready to move on to the deeper analysis of ideas for high school credit. If he's ready for deeper study when he's thirteen, set him loose. Once you teach your children to master the three skills of language, thought, and speech, the student can explore any number of ideas that excite his or her passions.

How will you do it?

Now, in my opinion, one of the most beautiful facets of a true classical education is the creative potential for a variety of learning experiences. Freed of previous requirements, you can choose any number of ways to teach your child the skills. Your objective is to teach a skill, but the classical method gives you the freedom and responsibility to teach that skill in any manner. This allows you to completely tailor the education to your child and family. Let's take an example.

General skill: Language

Specific skill: How to use nouns

Methods: Endless possibilities!

When teaching your child about nouns, you could go about it in any number of ways. You could have him listen to and memorize a grammar song about nouns. You could copy a paragraph from the book that he is reading and have him find all the nouns. You could have him substitute nouns in a well-written passage. You could take him on a field trip and have him identify all the nouns. You could read a passage, have him close his eyes, and have him say "noun" every time he hears you say one. You could have him make a list of all the nouns in a certain category. You could play a Scrabble game creating nouns. You could create a bingo game of nouns. You could create a thematic crossword puzzle of nouns. You could have him teach his little sister about nouns. You could toss a ball together while you alternate identifying nouns.

* * * * *

The potential for creative learning is only limited by your imagination and the Lord's inspiration. No longer bound to certain methods, curriculum, or artificial structure, you are free to teach the three skills of language, critical thinking, and communication in ways that uniquely meet the needs of your family. A true classical Christian education is not a cookie-cutter, one-size-fits-all formula. Take the three roads of the trivium, and recover your immense inheritance.

The First Road

&

Language

Chapter 7
Road Map for Mastery of Reading Skills

Theory is an interesting discussion, but we need precise instructions for turning the idea of an authentic classical Christian home education into reality. Navigating any journey requires planning the course from start to finish. That's why I have prepared my road maps for mastery of reading, thinking, and speaking skills. These checklists represent my personal goals for my children. You can use them as a springboard for developing your own goals.

In my opinion, these are the six specific language abilities that every literate child needs to master: (1) how to read, (2) how to spell, (3) how to write, (4) how to punctuate and capitalize, (5) how to use proper grammar, and (6) how to decipher unfamiliar vocabulary.

If you are one who needs more detail in achieving and assessing the skill, I have listed some basic abilities that I look for in my own children, but the list is certainly not all-inclusive. The beauty of classical education lies in the fact that you get to customize the content and methods to your own family's needs.

How to read
- Read aloud (from/to)
- Inflect voice
- Decipher phonetics
- Recognize sight words
- Read independently
- Narrate and predict content

How to spell
- Apply rules in context
- Find and correct errors
- Divide syllables and hyphenate
- Record dictation and correct errors
- Play spelling games
- Participate in spelling bees

How to write
- Learn lower and uppercase alphabet
- Create ABC book
- Refine print and cursive handwriting
- Copy classic authors
- Learn to type

How to punctuate and capitalize
- Learn rules of usage
- Add missing marks and capitalize
- Find and correct errors
- Learn proofreading marks

How to use proper grammar
- Memorize the eight parts of speech
- Substitute eight parts in context
- Learn gender, case, and declension of nouns
- Learn comparative and superlative rules of modifiers
- Learn conjugation of verbs
- Apply syntax rules
- Diagram sentences
- Familiarize with verbals

How to decipher unfamiliar vocabulary
- Interpret contextual meaning
- Practice dictionary usage

Please feel free to tailor this road map to your own needs. Simple goals allow us to teach out of a position of rest instead of anxiety. Keep your eyes on the big picture and be creative in achieving the goals.

Chapter 8
Learning the Language through Listening

The ancient Romans called this first skill set "grammar." The dictionary defines grammar as the system of rules governing the language which includes syntax (how sentences are put together), pronunciation (how letters and words are pronounced), semantics (what words mean), etymology (where words originated), and orthography (how words are spelled).

Hearing the Language

Your children have been acquiring the language ever since the day they were born. When they were young, you probably carried them on your hip and talked to them as you completed your daily tasks. You read picture books to them. You taught them the lyrics to silly songs. (I still remember a favorite: "If you wake up in the morning at a quarter to two, and you don't know just what to do...go brush your teeth!") You taught them nursery rhymes. You corrected their pronunciation when their first attempts were adorable misses. Hearing the language is the first step to proper pronunciation, pitch, rhythm, accentuation, and inflection.

But learning the language through hearing doesn't end with toddlers. I'm still learning the English language, and I've been hearing it for nearly half of a century! How do I learn the language through hearing? I listen to intelligent, challenging teaching CDs, watch quality movies or news programs, and engage in regular conversations with people who use good language like my husband and friends. Through hearing, I learn how to pronounce new vocabulary words and how to pace my conversations for maximum effect.

So what steps can you take to help your children learn the language through listening?

Read to them daily.

If they are still young, make reading out loud a daily tradition. Pick a time of day for all the kids to gather on the couch for a snuggle and a good picture or chapter book. If they are older and want to read the book on their own then read interesting newspaper articles to them around the table, or read a passage from the book that you are currently reading and share with them what you are learning!

If you have children of all ages, have the big brother or sister read daily to the little ones. One friend of mine has a son and two daughters. Both girls really enjoyed their special "sister time" when the teenage daughter read the American Girls series to her eight year old sister, while Mom taught their teenage son.

Listen to quality audio regularly.

We like to listen to books when we are traveling long distances in the car. G. A. Henty, a popular author of historical fiction, is particularly appealing to boys (probably because he always includes battles), and the vocabulary and sentence structure is always challenging. *Lamplighter Books* carries several audio versions of Henty by Jim Hodges.

Focus on the Family Radio Theatre classics like Les Miserables, The Secret Garden, and The Chronicles of Narnia are good choices that will engage your children's attention. My teens have also listened to sermons on CD (Doug Phillips of *Vision Forum*) and online (John Piper of *Desiring God Ministries.*)

For older teens who have substantially mastered the trivium, *The Teaching Company* offers countless opportunities to learn the specialized language of various disciplines like Biology, Advanced Mathematics, or Psychology.

Include them in conversations.

My kids learn more sophisticated language by eavesdropping! When David and I talk, we usually try to throw in a new vocabulary word or two just to keep the kids asking questions. They hear the way we structure our sentences and the way we pronounce those new words, and they naturally imitate what they hear. Socialize with other like-minded families who care about using proper language. The positive peer pressure will cause all the kids to speak with style.

* * * * *

One leading literacy expert states that ten year olds have a vocabulary ranging from 3,000 to 40,000 words! Do you know which kids have the

28

largest vocabulary? Of course you do! The kids with the greatest vocabulary are the ones who are regularly exposed to the spoken word through great literature and adult conversations. So if you want to raise classical scholars who have mastered the language, read to them and include them in conversations every day!

Chapter 9
Reading Aloud: the Key to Language Development

Parents who read aloud to their children contribute more to early language development than any other factor. Quantity and quality of literature plays a significant part in whether you will raise early readers or not. According to reading expert Marilyn Adams in *Beginning to Read*:

> "The most important activity for building the knowledge and skills eventually required for reading is that of reading aloud to children. In this, both the sheer amount of and the choice of reading materials seems to make a difference."

You want to raise classical scholars. The books your kids will be reading as teenagers and young adults are complex in both content and language: classic histories, philosophies, political treatises, scientific theories, and literature. Pave the way to future reading comprehension and enjoyment with these eight suggestions.

1. Read as often as possible.

The younger your child is when you begin reading to them the better! Make reading a daily tradition like brushing teeth. Read at bedtime, and read throughout the day whenever the kids ask for a story. Even if the entire day gets sidetracked due to unforeseen obligations or distractions, don't drop reading from the schedule. Sometimes when I've had to take care of emergencies, I've just told the kids to read until I can get back to them. Set aside time each day for the kids to read by themselves. Young children can "read" story books during naptime (even if all they are doing is looking at pictures and turning the pages), and older kids can read for 30 minutes once they're in the bed before lights are out. Show them that reading is a priority in your household.

2. Use real books.

Many home school convention vendors sell "readers" which are artificial stories built around phonics lessons. Please don't use these for your daily reading time! My experience with them is that they are rarely as entertaining and meaningful as "living" books. Use these phonics readers occasionally when you want to reinforce a phonetic sound. When the kids are young, start with colorful hardbound stories then move on to novels. As they get older, have Dad pick a great book to read aloud like a biography of an historical figure or original source documents like *The Declaration of Independence*. Even if the kids are reading on their own, try to incorporate some oral readings regularly.

3. Be patient as your child learns the art of listening.

Don't rush the reading. Take your time so that your child can hear all the sounds and point to all the words. This is an important step in acquiring the language as well as critical thinking. Kids who have not developed good listening skills rarely communicate effectively. Answer all their questions, and ask them some questions to train their listening abilities.

4. Put down a book that is clearly uninteresting.

Only read books that you both enjoy! Nothing is more miserable than slogging through a book that you both find boring. We all like different stories. Sometimes your home school friend may recommend a book that just doesn't appeal to your child. If you find your child yawning or unengaged, put that book down and find another one. In fact, let him choose the book that he wants to read.

5. Vary the length and subject matter.

Don't be too predictable. If the kids think that every time you sit down to read, they are going to have to endure hours of the same topic, they will begin to dread reading time. Keep them on their toes by doing the unexpected. One day read a story. The next day read a newspaper or magazine article. Then read a longer novel. Once you start the novel, you (and the kids) will likely want to keep going through the chapters until you finish the book. Next, vary the content by reading some poems. Read about all of life, not just "academics."

6. Plan enough time for questions.

Asking questions is the way classical home school parents teach. Don't tell them what the story means until after you've asked enough probing questions to determine their level of understanding. Let them try to figure it

31

out. Leave enough time for questions both before and after the reading. Before you get started with the story, look at the book jacket, inside cover, back cover, title page, pictures, and ask the kids to predict what the story is going to be about. Or with an older teen, have them look at the table of contents with you, and let them summarize the author's thesis. After reading, ask questions, too, about the characters, plot, events, or other meaning.

7. Express yourself.

Bland, dry reading is tortuous! Imitate the voices of actors who have pleasant reading voices (James Earl Jones, Jeremy Irons, and Meryl Streep come to mind) by adjusting your pace, pitch, and volume to fit the narrative. For instance let's say you are reading a scary scene where the character is worried about what's in the bedroom closet. Slow down and quietly whisper the words leading up to the climactic moment when the closet door is opened and the mystery revealed. Change your tone to match the content. Effective delivery makes all content more memorable.

8. Lead by example.

You know that our kids are great imitators. They are watching us all hours of the day, and they will naturally do what we do. So if you are not reading on a daily basis, don't expect to raise kids who love to read. Make sure that they see how important reading is to you. When we go to the library, I get a stack of books, too. Right now, I have 11 library books stacked up on my table three of which I have opened to passages that I'm comparing. When Meredith walked in a few minutes ago and asked me what I was working on, I was able to read a quick section to her and explain what I was learning. Plan little breaks in your day so that you can read for pleasure or for home school preparation. Share interesting things that you are learning from your reading, or let them hear you chuckling over a good passage.

* * * * *

In today's culture, reading is an integral element of gathering knowledge, understanding, and wisdom. Set your children on the road to discovery by reading aloud to them!

Chapter 10
What is the Purpose of Reading?

You might think that your child is translating the symbols on the paper into sounds in their head, but what he is really doing is translating the letters on the page into meaning. Comprehension is the goal of reading.

Learning the Structure

Do you remember those first board books that you used to read to your children? You'd hold your little one in your lap and point to the pictures and words as you read out loud. Perhaps you'd move your finger from left to right as the sentence progressed. Eventually your child began to point with you, and soon he excitedly "read" his favorite book to you! Why is learning to read so compelling? Because even the young child realizes that reading is not only fun, but reading is both useful and meaningful! The child learns that in the "hodge-podge of black on white is a story, somewhat like the stories that Dad tells at bedtime, but steadier and simpler in its variation of words and nuances. In its many rereadings, the story will become part of the child's world of imaginative experiences. And she will crave for ever more new ones." (Seymour Itzkoff, *Children Learning to Read*)

Reading is not just sounding out letters in perfect articulation. Reading is comprehending, understanding, or making sense out of the printed text. The search for meaning should be the primary purpose of reading. Even a colorful board book has meaning that the child can comprehend.

One of Meredith's favorite board books, *Goodnight Moon* by Margaret Wise Brown, is about a bunny who postpones bedtime by telling all the objects in the room "good night." In this example, the cute little bunny represents the little child, and the mama bunny represents the child's mother. Meredith may not have been able to verbalize her comprehension at the time, but she understood that, like the little bunny, she could try to stall bedtime, but eventually she would have to go to sleep. Likewise, sophisticated books, newspaper articles, and instruction manuals all have one final purpose: to convey meaning.

Seeing the printed text is an opportunity for learning the language. There are certain universal concepts about the printed word which every child needs to learn:

- print contains an exact message
- print can be letters and words which have individual sounds
- print corresponds one-to-one with the spoken word
- print progresses from left to right across the page and from top to bottom
- print progresses from the front page to the back page of a book

Children are incredible problem-solvers. For the youngest children, pictures act as clues to the meaning. As the books get more difficult, the pictures become less important, and the child has to determine the meaning of the passage from the text. Encourage your child to build a meaningful story in his head as he reads. Emphasize that every book has a lesson to be learned, a story to be told, or an event to relate so that over time he realizes that his foremost task in reading is understanding what he reads. In fact, problem-solving skills start with reading comprehension, so when you teach your children to look for meaning, you are helping them develop trivium skill number two, critical thought.

Understanding the Meaning

One of the hallmarks of a classical education is the use of Socratic Dialogue in which you ask the child what the text means instead of telling the child what the text means. I like to think in terms of "before, during, and after."

> Before - Ask LOTS of questions before you begin the book (and have your teen do the same!) by looking at the cover, the title page, and back cover. Flip through the pages and try to predict what the story will be about by browsing the pictures.

> During - Ask LOTS of questions as you are reading the story (or after each day's chapter for a teen). Find a good stopping place, and ask whether your predictions were correct? What will happen next? How will it end? (An older child is ready for more difficult questions about character analysis, plot, or cause and effect.)

> After – Once the story is over, have your child narrate the story back to you. Make sure he can tell you the beginning,

the middle, and the end. Teens should be able to identify the hero, villain, conflicts, climax, and moral or application to his own life. If you want to enrich their learning, occasionally have them write their understanding.

Teaching Inductive Reasoning

Another hallmark of classical home schooling is inductive reasoning. Consider the steps:

1. observe
2. interpret
3. apply

In the case of a book, your child observes the details of the story, interprets the meaning of the story, and then (you hope) applies the lesson learned. Back to my example of Meredith and *Goodnight Moon*: my toddler observed that on every page the little bunny said goodnight to the things in her room (observation). Then she understood that all little bunnies (and little girls) had to go to sleep even if they didn't want to (interpretation). Finally, she applied the lesson learned by allowing me to turn out the bedside light without a peep and tuck her in for a good night's sleep (application). When you teach your children to think inductively, you are on your way to developing understanding of the written word. This understanding is part of the foundation for critical thinking.

* * * * *

Like thought and speech, reading or literacy is a cumulative, ongoing process. Think of reading as a continuum of increasing competence. Classical scholars are lifelong learners who, once they have substantially mastered the tools of the trivium, are able to learn anything! Understanding the language involves determining the purpose or meaning of the written text as well as deciphering the code of the written text.

Chapter 11
Is Phonics Instruction Really Necessary?

Considering the sheer volume of available choices, phonics products have to be one of the most popular purchases that home school parents make! If you browse catalogs or the vendor booths at home education conventions, you'll agree. Games. Readers. Flashcards. Songs. Phonics product after phonics product woo parents with tempting promises like these:

"Provide the skills for children to become lifelong readers"

"A proven system that teaches children to read"

"Develop readers who can get meaning from print"

Rainbow Resource Center carries an astounding 410 different phonics products! Even respected mathematics giant, *Saxon Publishers*, offers two different phonics programs. According to economic theory, demand drives the supply, so home school parents must believe that phonics programs are necessary, but is this belief founded in reality?

Look-Say-Read?

For over a century, American educators have debated the usefulness of phonics instruction in teaching reading. Horace Mann introduced the "look-say" method where a child memorizes sight words instead of sounding out the letters. My own public school education in the 1960s utilized the famous look-say readers, *Dick and Jane* and their dog, Spot. I still remember reading "See Spot. See Spot run." Sight reading was the norm, but gratefully, my mother taught me how to sound out the letters and letter blends at home during our story time so that I became a proficient reader despite my public school education.

In 1955, reading and writing expert, Rudolf Flesch published a controversial book entitled *Why Johnny Can't Read* (later revised in 1981 in *Why Johnny Still Can't Read*) in which he proposed that phonics instruction was the missing link to American literacy. Flesch was considered a pariah and was ridiculed by the education establishment. In 1990 and 1997, the United States Congress commissioned studies to determine why public school kids couldn't read. Both reports concluded that phonics instruction was a necessary component of teaching reading and learning to spell. These findings indicate that although teaching sight words is helpful, phonics should be the primary method of learning to read.

Sound it Out

Instruction in phonics involves teaching kids to pronounce the sounds of letters first then the sounds of letter blends. Once the child knows how to pronounce the letters and the blends, he can effectively "sound out" any combination of single-syllable words and eventually move on to words with multiple syllables. In effect, phonics instruction teaches the alphabetic code, and once children know this code, they can effectively decode unknown words. For example, the child who learns the high frequency anchors (also known as roots or "rimes" by linguists) can change the first letter and build countless new words (the anchor "-ook" can become book, look, cook, and took).

* * * * *

So, it looks like all those home school parents purchasing phonics materials know something that public school parents don't know: phonics instruction is a necessary component of learning how to read. (Surprise, surprise!) One caution though...since authentic classical Christian education emphasizes literature over manufactured "readers" (those books that are in the phonics packages that are scripted around repeating certain letters and letter blends), use phonics instruction as a supplement to "living books." Don't substitute the phonics readers for real books. The kids will be bored and won't catch the excitement of a well-written story. And please don't start with flashcards and rote memorization drills. Start reading daily with young children and only introduce phonics after you've instilled a love for the written word!

Chapter 12
Practicing the Mechanics of Beginning Writing

Writing consists of two skills. First, the child practices the mechanics of developing correct letters and putting them together in properly spelled words, and secondly, the maturing child practices incorporating meaning into the composition.

Setting the Stage

You've been encouraging your child since birth to expand her spoken language abilities by surrounding her with music, conversations, nursery rhymes, and reading. You've gently corrected her when she made mistakes and always respond to her attempts to communicate with praise and excitement. You, your spouse, and her siblings are good role models in that you all love to read. She sees you reading all the time for pleasure and for learning. You read to her every day, and you answer every question with enthusiasm and maybe even more information than she wanted. You've looked at the pictures in the books and predicted the story plot line. You've shown her that the text moves from left to right and down by using your finger to point out occasional words. You've already taught her the alphabet song. You've diligently laid all the necessary groundwork of a rich, literate home where printed text is meaningful and pleasurable to read. Soon she'll be ready to acquire another critical skill of language development: writing!

Learning about Letters

Now that she can sing her ABCs reasonably well (even if she slurs the phrase "l-m-n-o-p"), it's time to start writing the letters of the alphabet. She may already know the names of some letters from your daily read-aloud time. You don't need to purchase an expensive curriculum to teach your child her ABCs. Just purchase an unlined art sketchbook with smooth paper, or go to the local copy shop and have them bind 100 pages with a spiral spine. You'll put one letter on each of 26 pages then later you'll add the letter blends like the sound "sh" and the sound "ck."

Start with her name. Teach her how to make the letters of her name by saying each letter as you write. Be very specific when you show her how to make each letter. For example, to make the uppercase letter "T" say something like "draw a straight line across" then "now find the middle of the line and draw a straight line down." Or when showing her how to draw the letter "B" say "start at the top and draw a straight line down" then "go back to the top and draw a fat tummy that points to the right and stops halfway" then "draw a 2nd fat tummy that starts at the center and also points right." Make sure you show her how to write both the uppercase and lowercase letter on the page. Be sure to use the words uppercase and lowercase instead of big and little when describing the letters.

Help her find pictures from magazines that start with each letter, or if you and she are good artists, draw a picture and color it like an apple for the letter "A." So now you have one page with the uppercase and lowercase letter and a picture or drawing of an object that starts with that letter. When you are finding pictures for the consonants, select images that sound like the single consonant and not a blend. For example, pick a "sock" for the letter "S" and not a "sheltie." You'll be adding photos or drawings of blends later.

In addition to working in your ABC book, use magnetic letters on the refrigerator, dry erase boards, doodle boards, paint, sand, or play letter games. You can make an easy BINGO board game on cardstock with the letters and letter blends, but don't just say the letter "D;" say "D as in dog." I really appreciated the DIY games in Peggy McKay's book, *Games for Reading*. Even as the kids got older, we played a reading game every Friday. Make learning the alphabet fun!

The Daily 30 Minute Workout

Now that she is becoming familiar with her ABCs, she is ready to begin reading out loud, narrating the story, and then writing her synopsis. This will probably be hardest for you because it will take longer, and it might be painful at first as she struggles with pronouncing and deciphering each word, but it is worth the effort! Continue reading out loud to her, but give her 30 minutes a day of dedicated reading time where she reads instead of you. Many parents discontinue read-aloud time once the child is reading by herself, but this is a big mistake. Children need to hear advanced readers speak difficult words and add inflection, pauses, and emphasis where needed.

Here are some constructive ways to spend that 30 minute daily reading and writing time. (Don't worry if you spend more than 30 minutes in the beginning…they'll pick up speed as they gain proficiency):

1. Select a familiar book that is below her reading level (easy).
2. Have her read the book out loud.
3. Select a new book that is slightly above her abilities (difficult).
4. Have her read this book out loud, too.
5. Work on a letter or letter blend in your ABC book, or play a game.

When you think she has mastered her ABCs (both upper and lowercase), you can introduce a handwriting book or purchase a handwriting pad at the local school supply store and create your own contextual words and sentences for her to copy as she practices writing.

Adding Narration, Dictation, and Copy Work through Stories

When you begin to notice progress, create another blank book for her stories and incorporate this step in the weekly routine:

Write a short story together. Let her generate the idea. In the beginning, have her dictate the story while you transcribe her words. Spell the word back to her before moving on to the next word. Repeat the entire sentence as it is completed. As she progresses in her skills, have her copy your dictation. Eventually, she can write her own story. (It can be one to two sentences long in the beginning.) When Daddy gets home, have her read her story aloud, and let him affirm her accomplishment.

Here are two possible options for constructing the narration book.

Option 1:

Take a blank piece of copy paper and turn it so that the short side (8 1/2") is at the top. Draw a horizontal line about 2/3 down the page. Then draw lines like wide-ruled notebook paper under the horizontal line to fill the bottom 1/3. First, she will write the story on the lines, and then she'll illustrate the story above the text. (This is also great for narrating and dictating daily Bible stories.)

Option 2:

Have the local copy shop bind 100 blank pages like the alphabet book, but this time use one side for the draft and the opposite side for the final, proofed text. Open the book flat, turn the book sideways so that the 11" side is at the top and have her write the first draft of the story on the top page. Have her read it and decide if she likes it the way it is. Gently correct any errors with a red pen, and add any new adjectives or details that she wants to add in red. Then have her recopy the edited draft on the bottom page. This is valuable groundwork for speech, the third skill of the trivium.

* * * * *

Before your child is ready for the advanced writing of skill number three, speech, teach her the mechanics of beginning writing. Eventually introduce cursive and later typing.

The Second Road

&

Thought

Chapter 13
Road Map for Mastery of Thinking Skills

Transforming the theory of a classical Christian home education into reality requires a pragmatic outline or, to continue the analogy of a journey along three roads, a precise map. Navigating any trip requires planning the course to reach the final destination. The following checklist represents my personal goals for helping my children master thinking skills. You may use this road map as a springboard for developing your own goals.

In my opinion, these are the seven primary thinking abilities that every literate child needs to master: (1) how to arrange data according to systems, (2) how to solve problems, (3) how to structure and analyze arguments, (4) how to use the scientific method, (5) how to analyze literature, (6) how to research a topic, and (7) how to listen.

For those of you who want more detail on how I assess the basic skills, I have listed my minimum requirements under each "how to" skill, but the list is certainly not all-inclusive. The beauty of authentic classical education lies in the fact that you get to customize the content and methods to your own family's needs.

How to arrange data according to systems
- Classify into categories
- Describe attributes
- Recognize similarities and differences
- Recall and relate patterns
- Reorder elements in a set

How to solve problems
- Identify and complete sequences
- Explain steps to creation or solution
- Associate and interpret analogies
- Memorize mathematical operations
- Understand and apply mathematical concepts
- Answer puzzles, riddles, and mysteries

The Second Road: Thought

How to structure and analyze arguments
- Identify claims and determine validity
- Distinguish difference between fact and opinion
- Build affirmative and negative positions
- Learn the deductive syllogism (if a & b, then c)
- Recognize common fallacies
- Practice inductive reasoning (observe, interpret, apply) with historical texts

How to use the scientific method
- Achieve familiarity with the general laws of science
- Understand difference between theory and fact
- Perform and document experiments
- Verbalize steps to observe, predict, and conclude

How to analyze literature
- Discover literary elements in whole works
- Identify literary techniques in portions of the whole work
- Diagram a narrative story chart from exposition to disposition
- Compare and contrast characters
- Identify and interpret themes

How to research a topic
- Select debatable idea
- Learn to use the internet and other hard reference works
- Determine credibility of experts

How to listen
- Focus on the live or recorded speaker with full attention
- Organize thoughts via outline or mental map
- Narrate understanding by asking questions or repetition
- Interpret meaning
- Answer questions precisely

Please feel free to tailor this checklist to your own needs. Simple goals allow us as parents to teach out of a position of rest instead of anxiety. Be creative in achieving your goals.

Chapter 14
Three Ways to Prepare Your Child for Logical Thinking

You've probably heard the Greek word "logos" used in a Christian sermon when the pastor, preaching from the Gospel of John, referred to Jesus as the "logos" or "Word" of the Father. According to a Greek Lexicon, the noun "logos" means "a word or discourse which embodies a conception or thought." The English word "logic" for which the second skill of the classical trivium is named derives from the Greek "logos" and is most commonly defined as the "study of formal reasoning." Therefore, one who studies logic is presumably capable of intelligent, reasoned thought and speech.

The Ancient Greeks understood the logic of the trivium as both (1) informal logic like the reasoned, methodical conversations between Plato's Socrates and his disciples and (2) formal logic as in the systematic principles of the syllogism (argument) of Aristotle. Socrates' leading questions helped his students understand why they believed what they believed, but he never told them what to think. Aristotle devised a deductive method for determining whether the premises and conclusion of arguments were sound or unsound.

The motivation for learning logic in ancient, medieval, and colonial times was simple: to distinguish between good and bad arguments so that thinking and the resulting oratory were more effective. Contemporary classical home school parents have their children study logic for the same reasons:

> To become critical thinkers who use language and reason to effectively communicate

But the study of formal logic is not the starting point for teaching thinking. That comes much later when the child is ready to handle abstract thought. So when do you start teaching your children to think? As soon as possible! Recent research points to the discovery that the brain's capacity for rational thinking and problem-solving is established by the age of one! Children whose parents have been actively speaking with them from birth have more complex networks of neurons which means they are predisposed to intelligence, creativity, and adaptability throughout life. In fact, John Chaffee, Ph.D., a pioneer in the field of critical thinking, states that "the number of words that an infant hears each day is the most important predictor of later intelligence, academic success, and social competence." Talk to your babies!

Children are full of energy, curiosity, and imagination which are all essential ingredients to critical thinking. Any parent knows that one of the favorite questions of children and teens is "Why?" Children explore. Children wonder. Children imagine. Here are three tips for nurturing your child's natural curiosity and expanding their minds:

1. Take their questions seriously.

> "Why do lightening bugs glow?"
> "Why does an onion make me cry?"
> "Why do bubbles burst when I touch them?"

Questions, questions, questions. Living with children brings never-ending questions, or so it seems. My 15 year old popped a doozy of a question on me about race and economics today after we volunteered in a downtown mission! Sometimes, you might be tempted to dismiss the constant questions because you are too busy or just too tired, but resist the easy way out. When you take your children's questions seriously, you are showing respect and validating their worth. Trust is built, and they feel secure in asking more questions without the fear of condemnation for being "silly" or "childish." What if they ask profound questions? We all want to protect our kids from the harsh realities of life, but don't avoid life's most difficult questions if you sense that they are mature enough to handle the answers. If you don't have the answers, confess your ignorance and commit to finding the answer with your teen.

2. Expose them to other perspectives.

When we look at issues from another person's perspective, we broaden our own understanding, recognize our bias, and gain new insights. This week the kids and I joined another home schooling family for some community service; our kids spent a couple of hours teaching hands-on science at a Christian mission in a very depressed area of town. After the workshop was over, I asked the neighborhood kids if they needed any help on their homework, and they excitedly pulled their assignments out. Each teen sat down with a child who was living in a different culture: different race, different economy, and different family life. But the Lord gives us the power to cross cultural barriers, and our kids connected with these children on a heart level. The little girl that Meredith was helping asked her to sit with her during the meal that followed.

As we drove home that evening, Meredith reflected on the disparity between the material poverty of this neighborhood and the extravagant wealth of the suburbs. Seeing life from that little girl's perspective had opened Meredith's eyes to a new reality. We've been serving as a family in inner-city missions for years, but for some reason, this was the day that my daughter really began to empathize on a deep level. Introduce other perspectives early and regularly because you never know when the "aha" moments will come, and a new understanding begins to take shape.

3. Talk about right and wrong.

I know I'm preaching to the choir on this one, but use every opportunity to train your children in righteousness. One of the key factors in critical thinking is knowing what you believe and why you believe it so that you can listen to others with different opinions and evaluate alternatives intelligently. Some of your child's most difficult questions will involve moral issues. For instance, in *Treasure Island*, Long John Silver is morally ambiguous. He is an unrepentant murderer and thief, yet he cares for Jim Hawkins and protects him from danger. How can someone who is bad do good things? Use literature and movies as opportunities to discuss good and bad, right and wrong.

Teach them why you believe what you believe. Explore Scripture for answers to their questions. Here's an example of a moral question that you might run across when you're reading Scripture. In *Exodus*, the midwives lie to Pharaoh's servants about the Israelite infants that they have secretly protected. Are there certain situations when the Lord allows deceit? Scripture is full of moral issues that you need to explore as a family so that the kids are ready to take a stand when analyzing other positions. Also make sure that you are 'walking the walk' as you are 'talking the talk,' too!

* * * * *

Questions are really just opportunities for stimulating discussion. Don't fall into the trap of thinking you need to answer all their questions. If you tell them what to think, you deprive them of the privilege of further thought and likely end the conversation. Many of life's most difficult questions don't have easy answers, so don't be afraid to say "I don't know" or to show your child how to discover the answer. Ask them questions!

Chapter 15
Top Ten Traits of a Critical Thinker

Children don't necessarily learn to think critically in public, private, or home schools. The U.S. educational model emphasizes "acquiring unrelated bits of information instead of developing a coherent framework of knowledge. But information is not knowledge. It doesn't become knowledge until the human mind acts on it and transforms it." (John Chafee, Ph.D., *The Thinker's Way*) According to the Greek playwright, Sophocles, "knowledge must come through action." In other words,

> The only way to become a better thinker is to think!

I have been privileged to know several critical thinkers in my life. Here are the top ten traits that I have observed in my friends who know how to think.

1. Critical Thinkers are Open-Minded

They listen carefully to every viewpoint, evaluating each perspective carefully and fairly. They recognize their own bias and are not afraid to hear other people's positions...in fact, they welcome hearing other viewpoints because then their own knowledge is broadened. They empathize with others.

2. Critical Thinkers are Knowledgeable

They have a broad knowledge base. Remember that knowledge is not the same as information...knowledge comes when you act upon the information by interpreting and applying it to your life. They base their opinions on facts, evidence, or personal experience. If they lack knowledge, they admit it.

3. Critical Thinkers are Mentally Active

They love the challenge of learning. They actively seek understanding and confront problems with glee. They do not respond to events or information passively. All of life is learning and acquiring new understanding. They are excellent observers.

4. Critical Thinkers are Curious

They have not lost the curiosity of their youth. One of their favorite questions is "Why?" They explore situations with probing questions that penetrate below the surface instead of being satisfied with easy answers.

5. Critical Thinkers are Independent

They don't borrow the ideas of others. They are not afraid to disagree with the crowd because they have developed their own opinion through thoughtful analysis and reflection. They can explain why they believe what they believe to be true.

6. Critical Thinkers are Conversationalists

They are skilled at discussing the issues in an organized and intelligent manner. Controversial issues don't scare them because they are good listeners who consider all the facts before responding.

7. Critical Thinkers are Insightful

They are able to get to the heart of the problem. They are not distracted by superfluous data. They can boil down an issue to the bare bones. They see the forest and the trees. They evaluate the accuracy of alternative positions and the credibility of their sources.

8. Critical Thinkers are Self-Aware

They know their own bias and are quick to point them out. They take their own position into consideration when analyzing a problem and look at all the alternatives equally.

9. Critical Thinkers are Creative

They are innovators who break out of established patterns of thinking. They imagine another way of solving the problem. They think outside of the box.

10. Critical Thinkers are Passionate

They have a passion for understanding. They are always striving to see the issues and problems with greater clarity. They engage in debates not for the purpose of proving their position "right" but to increase their own understanding.

* * * * *

Can you see the beginnings of a critical thinker in your own home school? Do you have a curious child? Does your child show great imagination? Do you have a listener in your family? Everybody thinks. The challenge is not producing thoughts but producing useful thoughts that are capable of changing their world for the better. Remember that a classical education teaches a child "how to think" not "what to think."

Chapter 16
What Does Your Child Need to Become a Critical Thinker?

Simply possessing information won't make your home school child intelligent. He needs to learn how to analyze, organize, evaluate, and apply information so that he can make intelligent judgments about daily life. The ancient Greeks and Romans didn't consider a person fully educated until the three skill sets of the classical trivium were mastered.

Language, road number one of the trivium, has the power to represent thoughts, feelings, and experiences using symbols. Therefore, language is the most important thinking tool your child has at his disposal. Language is not just for communicating but provides the structure for thought. That's why the ancients began the education with learning the primary language. The three skill sets of the trivium are related as follows:

Clear language that is specific, precise, and accurate results in clear thinking which is focused, coherent, and analytical which results in clear communication which is articulate, organized, and persuasive.

You should begin teaching the child to think before language acquisition is mastered. In Chapter 10, I recommended that you have the child orally narrate the meaning of the read-aloud story. This step is actually a critical thinking exercise! To be an active thinker, she has to use language to articulate an idea (the meaning of the story), evaluate the quality of the reasoning (is the child's narration based on the pictures and on the text?), and refine and improve the thinking process as you respond with leading questions for more understanding. In simpler terms, the child gathers information, processes the information, and creates meaning from the information:

1. Gather
2. Evaluate
3. Conclude

What does your child need to become a critical thinker? He or she needs keen observation, quality information, and analytical tools. Allow your child to work through problems, make mistakes, and improve over time. Developing critical thinking skills is a process not an event.

Keen Observation

Encourage your child to pay attention to details. When you take walks in the woods, stop and look at the creatures, the stones, and the decayed logs. Listen to the rustle of the leaves in the wind. Smell the fresh scent of dirt in spring. Touch the rough tree bark. Taste the sweet nectar of a golden honeysuckle. Ask lots of questions along the way. Teach him how the multiplication tables advance with each number so that he starts to see patterns. Talk about the details of the story that you're reading like character, setting, and conflict. Train him to ask probing questions and be patient when listening to others. As he ages, have him write about what he sees, hears, touches, smells, or tastes.

Quality Information

If the information is corrupted or inaccurate, a valid conclusion cannot be reached. Give him the best possible experiences and data. Train him to find quality texts at the library and bookstore. Teach him how to research, consider the credibility of authorities, and evaluate evidence. Expose him to alternative possibilities so that he learns to be open-minded and empathize with other people's perspectives even if he doesn't agree with them.

Analytical Tools

There are lots of tools for developing critical thinking skills. In the earliest years, start with storybooks and narration. Play lots of games, and work puzzles. Use manipulative objects when teaching mathematical concepts. Teach scientific concepts with hands-on activities. Ask questions throughout the day.

Around the ages of 9-12, introduce thinking matrices like *Mindbenders* by *Critical Thinking Press*. (My kids preferred the software to the books.) *Usborne* puzzle books were a favorite at this age, too. Sodoku puzzles range in difficulty and teach systematic analysis. Formal logic can be introduced for high school credit as early as 7th or 8th grade if your child is disciplined enough to tackle the formal syllogism. In my opinion, *Memoria Press* offers the clearest formal logic courses.

Learning how to structure a paragraph with a topic sentence and supporting sentences is another analytical tool that teaches organization skills. Older kids should be writing their observations and interpretations. According to Holocaust survivor, Elie Wiesel, "I write to understand as much as to be understood." Writing helps clarify our thinking.

* * * * *

Finally, in order to raise a critical thinker, you need to model critical thinking yourself! Demonstrate critical thinking on a regular basis. When you read the newspaper editorials, discuss the issues with the kids and point out bias, alternative perspectives, and possible solutions. If he is stuck on a math problem, sit down and work on it together. Walk him through the steps of analysis. Teach her how to write up a scientific laboratory observation and conclusion. Share what you are learning and thinking about the book or magazine that you are reading in your personal time. Do you keep a written journal of your learning? Show the kids so they can see how important critical thinking is to you. Model the behavior, and provide the tools that they need to practice, and soon you'll have young adults who know how to express a clear thought in an influential and persuasive manner.

Chapter 17
Know Why You Believe What You Believe

"I don't know."

Perhaps you thought you understood a concept then when pushed to summarize the concept in a clear, concise statement, you found yourself uttering the feeble words "I don't know." Or maybe you asked your son to explain what he just read, and he weakly stammered "I don't know." If you can't explain why you know something, then you don't really know it!

The English word "critical" derives from the Greek word "kritikos" which means to question, to make sense of, or to analyze. Critical thinkers know why they believe what they believe because they have asked lots of questions, analyzed lots of data, and have made sense of the evidence. According to *Merriam Webster*, a belief is "a conviction of the truth of some statement or the reality of some being or phenomenon especially when based upon examination of evidence." In evaluating beliefs, we need to consider four different kinds of evidence: expert authorities, written references, hard facts, and personal experience.

Expert Authorities

An authority is one who is an expert in a field and has usually devoted the majority of his working career to gaining a deep understanding of his area of expertise. Biblical scholars specialize in interpreting particular books of the Bible. Supreme Court justices specialize in Federal Constitutional Law. Anthropologists specialize in indigenous cultures. Who are the authorities for your core beliefs? Are they particularly knowledgeable in the area of the belief? Are they reliable? Have they ever given inaccurate information? Do other authorities have a basis for disagreement?

Written References

Original source documents like books, newspapers, and online publications are written by authors who could be authorities or work for authorities. What texts do you rely upon to support your beliefs? Is the content of these texts based upon factual evidence? What are the credentials of the authors? How much personal experience does the author have with the topic? Does the author have a relationship with someone who is an authority on the topic? Are there other authors who disagree with the position that your texts endorse? Is there evidence to support the opinion of these texts?

Hard Facts

Facts are pieces of information presented as having objective reality; that is, facts can be objectively quantified or substantiated and are not subject to the interpretations of the user. When considering the facts behind your beliefs, inquire of the source of the facts. Were experiments performed to statistically quantify the facts? Was evidence obtained to substantiate the conclusions? Can this evidence be interpreted differently? Does the factual evidence support the conclusion?

Personal Experience

Many times our beliefs are based upon personal experiences. In evaluating these experiences, ask yourself the following questions. What were the circumstances of the experience? Were distortions or mistakes in perception possible? Have other people had similar or conflicting experiences? Are there other explanations for the experience?

You don't have to examine each of these four types of evidence for every belief or position that you consider, but critical thinking skills will be improved if you practice asking these questions regularly. Think of a core belief that you hold about life then go through this exercise step by step. Some possible beliefs that you could examine are what you believe about marriage, parenting, or home schooling. Here are the steps:

1. Describe the belief.
2. Explain why you feel so strongly.
3. Identify evidence for your position.
4. Describe an opposing point of view.
5. Identify evidence for the opposing viewpoint.
6. Evaluate the evidence for both positions:
   a. Who are the authorities?
   b. What are the written references?
   c. What are the facts?
   d. What are your personal experiences?

Was that difficult to do? Now you're ready to try this exercise with your child. Select an easy belief to start with then move on to more difficult beliefs. For instance, in my household, *Handel's* homemade ice cream is favored above all other brands, so I might guide the kids through the following analysis:

1. Describe the belief. (*Handels* is the best ice cream brand.)

2. Explain why you feel so strongly. (great flavor, huge variety, creamy texture, and fair price)

3. Identify evidence for your position. (personal experience, newspaper articles, and traffic)

4. Describe an opposing point of view. (*Ritter's* frozen custard is a better frozen treat.)

5. Identify evidence for the opposing viewpoint. (Some people prefer the lighter, creamier texture of custard as evidenced by all the cars parked in front of the building.)

6. Evaluate the evidence for both positions:
    a. Who are the authorities? (regular neighborhood customers)
    b. What are the written references? (newspaper testimonials)
    c. What are the facts? (nutrition statistics available)
    d. What are your personal experiences? (weekly visit)

You can use these tools to evaluate all kinds of beliefs from moral positions (like "I believe lying is wrong") to scientific theories (like "I do not believe global warming is a threat to the earth") to difficult worldview issues (like "I believe in the Trinity"). Start with the easier concepts from their math lessons (like "I believe nine times eight is seventy-two" or "I believe a right triangle has one 90 degree angle") or from their history reading (like "I do not believe the American Civil War was caused by slavery" or "I believe that Benedict Arnold was a traitor").

* * * * *

You might want to set aside a few minutes every morning to practice this exercise just like you would practice an impromptu speech. Give the kids a topic (abstract ideas like love and power or concrete ideas like evolution and property ownership), and set the timer for ten minutes. Give them a note card and have them complete the six steps above. When the timer goes off, have them narrate their thoughts from the note card. I promise you that this exercise will stimulate their thinking; it really reveals how much they do or do not know about their belief! Train your kids in how to evaluate their beliefs so that they can confidently give a precise, thoughtful answer next time when you ask them why they believe what they believe.

Chapter 18
Can a Critical Thinker Be Creative, Too?

Absolutely yes! The second road, "Thought," involves giving your children tools to solve problems. Observation, language, and evidence are all components of critical thinking, but so is creative thinking. How is creative thinking related to critical thinking?

To be a creative thinker is to have a sense of discovery…to imagine…to invent…to be curious. Critical thinkers need to foster creative thinking so that they can develop viable alternatives and solutions for the problem. Solving problems involves the following five steps:

1. Identify the real problem.
   - a. Ask lots of questions.
   - a. Who? What? When? Where? Why? How?
   - b. What is causing the problem?
   - c. Eliminate the distracting side issues.

2. Generate a list of alternatives.
   - a. Consult experts.
   - b. Brainstorm.
   - c. Set the timer and "jam" random thoughts.
   - d. Imagine new ways of doing it.
   - e. Postpone judgment until later.

3. Evaluate the pros and cons of your possible solutions.
   - a. What do the experts recommend?
   - b. What do the written references say?
   - c. What are the facts?
   - d. Do you have personal experience?

4. Decide on the best solution.
   - a. What pros and cons can you merge?
   - b. What alternative solutions can you eliminate?
   - c. What is the most workable solution?

5. Monitor the results of your plan.
   - a. How well is your solution working?

b. Did anything unexpected happen?

c. Are there any adverse effects?

To think creatively about a problem, your child has to develop a deep understanding of the central concept and issues. In order to foster an environment where creative thinking is encouraged, provide the following conditions in your home school.

Time

Allow lots of uninterrupted time with no distractions so that your child can really think about the issue. Give less work so that he or she can go deep. Eliminate distractions (I know this is difficult). Give him time to concentrate so that those creative juices flow. He needs time to absorb all the facts of the situation and imagine solutions.

Place

You've probably heard this before, but we really do need a quiet place to engage in deep thinking. My kids work all over the house, both inside and outside, but when they need to really concentrate, they go to their "quiet places." Meredith goes to her room and closes the door, and Connor disappears in the study. There's also some value in going to the same quiet place each time they want to do some serious thinking because every time they reenter that place, the memory of prior "ah hah" moments will trigger a similar eureka moment this time.

* * * * *

So where does creative thinking factor into these five problem-solving steps? People who think creatively come up with alternatives and solutions that are not the norm. Creative thinkers illuminate the crux of the problem. Creative thinkers innovate when it comes to alternatives. Creative thinkers imagine a better solution. Once a little creativity has been applied to the problem, a critical analysis of the problem, alternatives, and solution can be performed. The more creative thinking your child does, the more ideas he'll produce. The more creative ideas your child produces, the more skilled he'll become. The more skilled he becomes, the more satisfying his sense of accomplishment will be. The more satisfying his accomplishments, the more he will love learning!

Chapter 19
Why Writing Is a Catalyst to Intellectual Development

Pulitzer prize-winning American author, Annie Dillard, is quoted as saying,

> "I don't know what I think until I see myself write."

Writing down your thought processes is a necessary step to a fuller understanding of the problem, issue, or idea. Simply listening to a news program, a sermon, or a lecture is not enough. Let's consider a common scenario.

While you're watching a news program with your husband, the telephone rings, and he leaves to go answer the call. When he returns, he asks you what he missed. You might be able to immediately reconstruct the basics of the story, but would you be able to accurately recount the details a week later? Now let's assume that the next evening, you decided to take notes during the broadcast. I'll bet if you compared your recap from both nights, you would clearly see the benefit of writing down your thoughts.

Why is writing a catalyst to intellectual development in your home school?

The process of writing:

- stimulates the mind
- improves memory
- shapes critical thinking
- enlarges understanding
- provides a permanent record

Writing Stimulates the Mind

You've probably heard that you'll retain information more effectively if you give it to your brain by more than one method. When your child reads a book, she is gathering information and storing it using visual cues. When your daughter then narrates what she learned in the book, she is organizing and storing that information a second time using auditory cues. Finally, when she writes while she is reading or even after she has read a passage, she is storing that info using both touch and sight. This child has now engaged the same information three different ways, and she is very likely to have a better understanding than she would have if all she had done was read the chapter.

Writing Improves Memory

Not only does processing information using multiple methods improve understanding, but it also improves memory. Since the late 1960s, leading memory authorities have documented the fact that organizing information into categories makes the info more memorable thus more likely to be retained in long-term memory. Additionally, writing down your thought processes or ideas usually results in a mental picture of the outline, sketch, or notes so that when you need to recall the information, you can readily remember your written notes by calling up your internal "teleprompter."

Writing Shapes Critical Thinking

In order to write some thought down on paper or to type the thought on the computer keyboard, we need to first organize the information. We are forced to reduce all the incoming data to determine the main problem and identify the solution. Does your child have trouble with math word problems? My kids used to struggle with word problems until I showed them how to circle the important facts in the problem then translate the words into a mathematical equation or formula. As they dissected the word problem, they were able to focus on what the problem was asking and come up with the correct solution.

Writing Enlarges Understanding

When we exclusively confine our learning to reading or hearing someone else's interpretation, we miss out on greater understanding. When we choose to write down the facts and come to our own conclusions, we inevitably stumble upon concepts that we thought we understood but later realized that we did not really grasp the problem. So, we've got to dig a little deeper to clarify our own understanding. Meredith and I watch a DVD on biology, and as we each draw our own "branch" outlines of the lecture, we often pause the DVD to discuss concepts that we don't understand.

Writing Provides a Permanent Record

As home educators, we need to keep certain records in order to comply with the state. You also might want to keep a written record of your kids' work in case they decide to home school their kids and need to refer back to their own home school work! At the end of the academic year, I ask the kids to pull their favorite examples from each area of study so that I can incorporate those writing samples in their portfolio or scrapbook.

I keep reading journals (three ring binders or spiral notebooks) for all of my own studies. It is especially rewarding to go back through my "Quiet Time" Scripture journals from over the years and see how I am growing in my understanding and relationship with Jesus. I also keep my history, literature, and science notebooks in case I ever want to go back and consult them. They are really a "history" of who I was at that place and time because they reflect those thoughts and questions that I found most important.

* * * * *

Here's a quick exercise for you and the kids. Select an article out of the newspaper. Have the oldest child read it and narrate the main points to the rest of the family. Appoint one family member to take notes of what the narrator said. Then have the oldest child read the article again, but this time have him or her write down thoughts before narrating. Have the secretary take notes again. Compare the two accounts of the article. Which account reflected a greater understanding of the topic?

Chapter 20
Shiver Me Timbers! Do I Have to Teach Logic?

Formal Logic…most of us never learned the rules in school and shudder at the very thought of teaching it! But if you are going to raise a classical scholar in your home school, you really need to become familiar with the concepts and terms. In fact, you may find after completing a few lessons that you actually enjoy this methodical way of constructing and evaluating arguments. Here is an overview of the study of logic in laymen's terms.

History

The western version of classical logic originated in classical Greece with Aristotle. He called his argument the "syllogism." Each statement followed a particular order containing a subject and a predicate. There are many vocabulary words, but three important ones to remember when teaching logic are: argument, reason, and conclusion.

Method

Reasoning shapes our thinking into intelligent patterns. When someone asks us for our reason for believing something, our minds have to go beyond the information given in order to decide, explain, predict, or persuade. Our reasons support our conclusion. So, a simple definition of logic is:

The system for using reasons and conclusions to construct and evaluate arguments

Whenever we give reasons to support our conclusions, we are presenting an argument. Officially, such reasons are called "premises." Here's the structure:

Reason 1 (evidence #1 to justify the conclusion)

Reason 2 (evidence #2 to justify the conclusion)

Conclusion (explains, asserts, or predicts based on evidence)

Here's a real-life example of a formal argument:

> Murder is against the law.
>
> Destroying human embryos is murder.
>
> Therefore, destroying human embryos is against the law.

Traditional logic teaches methods for evaluating criteria like validity, truth, and soundness. Anthony Weston provides a brief overview of logic in his *Rulebook for Arguments* if you want an executive or top-level summary of the subject. In our own home, we've used two logic curricula: *Canon Press* and *Memoria Press*. My recommendation would be to purchase *Memoria Press' Traditional Logic*, books 1 and 2, for a full year of high school credit. Most kids are ready to tackle this methodical workbook sometime between the 7th and 8th year of formal academics.

* * * * *

Critical thinking will skyrocket once your kids begin to understand traditional logic. In lesson five of the second semester of the *Memoria Press* text, they learn how to apply all the methods for constructing and evaluating arguments to real-life. They can then take any newspaper article, identify the arguments including premises and conclusions, and evaluate with specific tools whether the argument is sound or not. This is a critical thinking skill that is rare in our culture and certainly unusual among teenagers; you owe it to your kids to give them these tools so that they are ready to take what they've determined and communicate their position effectively.

The Third Road

&

Speech

Chapter 21
Road Map for Mastery of Speaking Skills

My three road maps for mastery of reading, thinking, and speaking skills are meant to provide a framework for assessing mastery of the three roads of the classical trivium. These checklists represent my personal goals for my children. You can use them as a starting place for developing your own goals.

In my opinion, there are five primary communication abilities, both oral and written, that every literate child needs to master: (1) how to maintain a conversation, (2) how to write a paragraph, (3) how to take notes, (4) how to write advanced compositions, and (5) how to give a speech.

Under each "how to," I have listed some basic content ideas, but the list is certainly not all-inclusive. Remember that the beauty of an authentic classical education lies in the freedom to customize the content and methods to your own family's needs.

How to maintain a conversation
- Look at people when conversing
- Shake hands firmly and repeat their name
- Listen intently
- Answer the telephone and take a message
- Draft personal, business, and email correspondence
- Follow manners, etiquette, and protocol in social situations

How to write a paragraph
- Write a topic sentence
- Support the topic in remaining sentences
- Vary sentence structure
- Add stylistic elements
- Incorporate transitions
- Clinch the title from the final sentence
- Imitate classic authors by substituting words
- Practice using thesaurus

How to take notes
- Outline main points of text and lecture

- Annotate in book margins
- Construct an abstract or summary from notes
- Narrate understanding
- Reduce notes to main ideas

How to write advanced compositions
- Develop a hook to gain attention
- Draft introductions and conclusions
- Vary paragraph style
- Learn the basic three point essay
- Develop a thesis statement
- Research and gather evidence to support thesis
- Cite authorities via footnotes
- Create bibliography
- Present and defend oral dissertation
- Proofread and edit every composition

How to give a speech
- Memorize, recall, and recite stories, scripts, and speeches
- Punctuate points with eye contact and body language
- Gain platform experience (expository, persuasive)
- Gain interpretive experience (dramatic, humorous, and duo)
- Gain limited prep experience (impromptu, apologetics, extemporaneous)
- Acquire team policy debate experience
- Analyze famous historical speeches for form and style

Please feel free to tailor this road map to your own need. Add or subtract according to your personal objectives. Teach out of a position of rest instead of anxiety by keeping your communication goals simple. Keep your eyes on the big picture and be creative.

Chapter 22
Words Have the Power to Change the World

Not long ago, I witnessed the trial of a first-time juvenile offender. Furious with his mom for refusing to drive him to his girlfriend's house, this young man demolished the back window of her truck. His frustrated parents pressed charges, and he soon found himself in front of a judge and a jury on the witness stand. Regrettably, this in itself is not unusual in our culture; however what I found most astonishing and disturbing was the manner in which this young man communicated with his interrogators: grunts!

Single word grunts issued from his scowling lips. He was extremely disrespectful towards the judge and showed no indication of repentance or remorse. The judge had to ask the young man to respond in complete sentences! But the real shocker came when the jury was dismissed to deliberate: both parents began an eloquent conversation with the court officials. Clearly, his parents were well-educated and effective communicators. How did this young man end up with such a deficiency in communication skills? Do we run the same risk as these parents? Is it possible that our children, when faced with unexpected situations, will find themselves answering in one word replies? Do we take effective communication skills for granted?

Christians are called to more than grunts! We seek to glorify God in every word and deed. Colossians 3:17 succinctly summarizes our responsibility as Christians:

> "And whatever you do, in word and deed, do everything
> in the name of Jesus, giving thanks to God the Father
> through Him." (NRSV)

What does it mean to speak every word in the name of Jesus? Let's look at the term "word" in Scripture. The Gospel of John refers to Jesus as the Word of the Father, and the Old Testament prophets regularly delivered the "Word" of Yahweh to the King. The Creator reaches out to the creature and communicates, through spoken words like those delivered to the prophets, through invisible encounters as in the apostle Paul's conversion story, through the written word of the canon of Scripture, and finally

73

through the incarnation of Jesus. The Word of the Lord is of utmost importance because it is through that Word that the Living God reveals who He is for the sake of a full relationship with us. Communication is vital to our relationship with Him and with others, so we, as little "Christ-bearers," recognize that our words, whether written or spoken, are also meant for relationship with others, and as such, they have the power to change lives. We speak in Jesus' name as He would speak...in truth, in love, and with a mind toward advancing His Kingdom.

As classical home schooling parents, we have a deed to do: train our children in effective communication skills. They may have a true desire to speak every word in Jesus' name, but if they don't have the tools, their efforts may not reach full potential. In order to influence others effectively, our children must marshal the language, seek out the best arguments, and organize ideas with compelling style and captivating delivery. Equipped with the necessary skills, our eloquent children will respond to difficult questions with thoughtful, persuasive words that, unlike base grunts, have the power to change the world!

Chapter 23
Could You Define Classical Rhetoric?

According to the honorable Zell Miller, former governor of the state of Georgia and United States Senator,

> "Twenty years of votes can tell you much more about a man than twenty weeks of campaign rhetoric. Campaign talk tells people who you want them to think you are. How you vote tells people who you really are deep inside."

Although you've heard the word "rhetoric" used in contemporary conversations, you might not have a clear idea of what it means in terms of an authentic classical education. The two most common usages of the word rhetoric in my community of Christians are as follows: (1) the inflated verbosity of politicians to win votes at all costs, and (2) the misuse of the original term to describe a "stage" of classical home education, generally the high school years. Our lack of understanding stems from the fact that the term rhetoric belongs to an art (remember the "seven liberal arts" of a classical education?) that was constructed during ancient times, practiced for thousands of years, yet abruptly abandoned as a fundamental discipline in our public schools during the middle to late 1800s. In short,

Rhetoric is the art of oratory.

For thousands of years, classical rhetoric was classified as (1) verbal, (2) conciliatory, (3) persuasive requests (as opposed to coercive demands) that were (4) delivered by a single orator. More recently with the invention of the printing press, the term rhetoric was broadened to include written as well as spoken oratory. Oratory, derived from the Latin infinitive "orare," which means "to pray", is simply the art of speaking in public and writing for the public. The same principles of rhetoric are applied to both oral and written disciplines.

Classical rhetoric is the art or discipline of using written and spoken discourse to persuade, inform, or motivate an audience…the very essence of the speech or essay is meant to move the listener or reader. According to Scottish Presbyterian Minister and Master of Rhetoric, George Campbell,

"We discourse to enlighten the understanding, to please the imagination, to move the passions, or influence the will."

Although Campbell was primarily interested in the art of rhetoric because he believed it would result in better preachers, contemporary home school parents see the application of rhetoric to a whole slew of opportunities from platform, interpretive, and limited preparation speeches to books, sermons, and face-to-face encounters in the community.

* * * * *

Classical rhetoric, simply put, consists of three steps: (1) the idea, (2) the proof, and (3) the call to action.

Chapter 24
Rhetoric in a Nutshell: Idea, Proof, and Call to Action

Rhetoric is the art of oratory. Today we generally refer to oratory as "public speaking" or "speech;" however, I think you'll agree that the principles of rhetoric can be appropriately applied to written communication like essays, research papers, and even journalism articles. Other than impromptu speeches, which happen on the spur of the moment with limited preparation time, most contemporary speeches start with a written script or at least an outline of the speaker's (1) idea or claim, (2) proof or evidence, and (3) call to action. So for our purposes, I'll define rhetoric as:

> A system for gathering, selecting, arranging, and expressing our material whether in oral or written form

Remember that rhetoric is one of the "seven liberal arts" of ancient Rome. If you were to examine the other six liberal arts (language, logic, geometry, astronomy, music theory, and arithmetic), you would realize that each of these arts involves a system for gathering, selecting, arranging, and expressing the material.

Let's modernize this concept. You could probably list a vast number of "arts" that also involve a system for accumulating, organizing, and presenting the material. For instance, the "art of cooking" involves deciding on the recipe, gathering the ingredients, combining the ingredients in a certain measure and order, cooking the mixture, arranging the final presentation, and serving the delightful dish to the audience. In a nutshell, the chef has concocted an idea, presented evidence to prove her idea, and announced a call to action: "eat and enjoy!" The art of gardening, the art of sewing, and the art of singing are just three examples that follow a similar pattern of idea, proof, and call to action. Likewise, the master writer or orator develops an idea, presents the evidence, and calls the audience to action.

In other words, rhetoric for the classical home school is not a stage of educational progress, but rather a set of procedures and criteria that guide the author or orator in making strategic decisions during the composition process. During ancient and medieval times, this system was tightly defined as three kinds of persuasive discourse: deliberative, forensic, and epideictic oratory.

Chapter 25
Classical Discourses: Three Ways to Persuade

During ancient and medieval times, classical rhetoric was strictly defined in one of three ways: deliberative oratory, forensic oratory, or epideictic oratory. I prefer to call these three kinds of classical discourse by their function: political, legal, and ceremonial speeches. Although these are ancient forms of communication, they are still practiced effectively today in the public realm. Here's a quick primer for you:

Political Oratory

The term "deliberative" oratory originates with usage; elite orators deliberated over public affairs such as whether to go to war, whether to raise taxes, whether to enter alliances, and whether to construct infrastructure like bridges and baths. The point of deliberative (political) oratory was to persuade the audience to do something or accept a certain point of view. Concerned with the future (either we will or will not do it), political orators focused on expediency (the opportunity is now...let's do it) and inexpediency (it is not wise or prudent to take this action) by exhorting (strongly urging) and dissuading (advising against) the audience.

Deliberative oratory is still practiced today in the U.S. Capitol, the White House, and in state and municipal centers around the country. Home school teenagers who participate in local, regional, and national debate competitions engage in deliberative oratory as they seek to persuade the judge to adopt either the affirmative or negative position.

Legal Oratory

The term "forensic" is often used in relation to crime scene evidence, but the Latin root of forensic is actually "forum" which was the central gathering place in ancient cities where judicial and public business was discussed. Public speakers who delivered forensic or legal oratory usually advocated the defense or condemnation of individuals and their related actions. Unlike deliberative or political orators, forensic orators are concerned with the past. That past could be crimes committed, charges unjustly brought, or behavior that needs public reckoning. Topics most often addressed were justice and injustice by means of accusation or defense.

Today's forensic oratory is most often heard in courtrooms as attorneys plead the cases of their clients before judges. In fact, law schools still consistently teach a variation of this classical discourse.

Ceremonial Oratory

Epideictic, a Greek derivative, means "for display," so it shouldn't surprise you that I choose to call this type of classical discourse "ceremonial." Demonstrative or declamatory in nature, the ceremonial speech intends to please, to inspire, to entertain, or to shame. Concerned with the present, topics most often include honor or dishonor. The means by which the ceremonial orator got his message across were either praise or blame. The nature of the speech lends it to literary style more so than the other two kinds of classical discourse.

Although politicians often find themselves using this speech when introducing their superiors (praise) or their rivals (blame), we most often hear this kind of discourse at celebrations like Fourth of July Parades, Memorial Day Services, and other public ceremonies. Pastors often employ this style even though they also use the deliberative discourse to encourage their congregation to do the right thing. The Gettysburg Address is a contemporary example of a ceremonial speech.

To summarize, the three kinds of classical discourse are:

Political Oratory:
1. The Point: to persuade for action or inaction
2. Concern: the future
3. Topics: expedient and inexpedient
4. Means: exhortation and dissuasion

Legal Oratory:
1. The Point: to defend or condemn
2. Concern: the past
3. Topics: justice and injustice
4. Means: accusation and defense

Ceremonial Oratory:
1. The Point: to please, inspire, entertain, or shame

2. Concern: the present
3. Topics: honor and dishonor
4. Means: praise and blame

* * * * *

If you think about who delivered these three types of classical discourse in the past and what positions they held in society, you quickly see that they were all societal leaders. Politicians, legislators, executives, lawyers, judges, pastors, and others of importance to the community employed the systematic tools of classical rhetoric to impact their culture in significant ways. If you hope to raise leaders, then you need to consider how classical rhetoric factors into your plans for teaching effective communication.

Chapter 26
Socratic Dialogue:
Leading Questions Illustrated

Communicating effectively is not limited to classical discourse like formal speeches or written compositions. Narration is a communication skill that is used in casual conversation more than the other two combined! Think about the countless times during a day that you ask your child questions...

- How did you sleep last night?
- What did you dream about?
- What are your plans for study today?
- What was the book about?
- What would you like for dinner?
- How did you spend your free time this afternoon?
- What do you want to be when you grow up?
- What did you learn from your reading?

Moms and dads are great at asking questions! But the risk with asking open-ended questions is that you'll get vague responses like "okay" (how did you sleep), "I can't remember" (what was the book about), and "I don't know" (what did you learn today). What you want to do as a classical home educator is draw out your child's understanding so that he or she is giving you more than one-word grunts. You know that words have the power to change the world, and you want to raise world-changers who are eloquent and persuasive! Train them in giving concise, direct answers so that when they find themselves out in the community and someone asks a question, they are prepared.

So how do you coax your reluctant child to give thoughtful responses to your questions? Socratic Dialogue is one method that we use in our home school to great effect especially in the high school years. Why is it so effective during the teenage years? By the time most children reach their teens, they are ready to grapple with abstract concepts like truth and liberty. The two-way dialogue between a knowledgeable parent and a tender-hearted teen fosters deeper understanding about difficult concepts.

In our family, we consider Socratic Dialogue a key tool of an authentic classical education, but because we were not exposed to this kind of questioning in our own youth, it took a little practice before we were comfortable asking directed questions. Start practicing now by asking specific questions with your younger children so that you are ready when the big ideas are discussed during the teen years.

Remember that Courtroom Drama?

Unless you are a practicing attorney, you probably haven't had a lot of experience in using Socratic Dialogue. In fact, attorneys (and some home school students) are the only living Westerners who still use this classical tool. Attorneys receive training in Socratic Method in law school where they learn to ask leading questions of a witness.

If you have ever been to a legal deposition or watched a courtroom drama, you know that a good prosecutor asks leading questions. In preparation for the trial, the attorney "deposes" the witness. In a deposition, the attorney asks the witness pertinent questions under oath, and a court transcript is created which both the defending and prosecuting teams receive. In deposing the witness, the attorney is trying to arrive at the facts of the case. These facts are the basis for the trial, and a skillful attorney will use these facts in asking leading questions of the witness so that the witness gives him the answers that he wants. Facts are the starting point for your Socratic Dialogue preparation, too.

What are the FACTS?

Just like the attorney, you need to know the facts before you can ask useful leading questions. Unless you are already an expert on the subject matter, you need to read the material along with your child. Now I am not saying that you have to read every single word that the child reads; if you have more than one child, the task of keeping up with all of the weekly reading assignments plus all of your other family responsibilities would be overwhelming! Be selective. You might choose one subtopic from your teenage daughter's science reading, one chapter from your preteen son's history reading, and one picture story book to read with your youngest child. By the way, the Socratic Method works well with both fiction and nonfiction.

Select the Process to be Described

One of the easiest ways to practice this method with young children is to select a process to explain. I think of this as the "how to" dialogue. Pick something that she already knows about, or pick some topic from the current reading. Before you begin, study the process so that you are familiar with the steps to completion. Here are a few possible ideas for discussing a familiar process:

- How to build a model rocket
- How to braid a sister's long hair
- How to give the dog a bath
- How to score a football game
- How to bake cookies

You could also select a process from the science reading like how to inflate a balloon inserted on a 2 liter bottle. Instead of a process, you could select an item and ask her to describe the component parts from top to bottom.

Plan the Leading Questions

Once you've got your topic, you can now plan the questions. Think in terms of detailed steps. What are the steps to giving the dog a bubble bath? Brainstorm and put the steps in order from first to last like this:

1. Find the shampoo
2. Ask Mom for an old towel
3. Get the bucket
4. Take the bucket, shampoo, and towel to the back yard
5. Turn on the hose
6. Pour the water into the bucket
7. Find the dog and bring him to the bucket
8. Wet the dog's body
9. Put shampoo in hand
10. Lather and scrub the dog all over
11. Rinse the dog
12. Dry the dog off
13. Stand back as he shakes the water all over you!

You now have the answers to leading questions such as "what liquid would I use to clean the dog's fur?" Another approach could be "tell me what order you would follow to give the dog a bath." You don't have to be this formal every time. Leading questions can be asked casually when you are in the car, at the breakfast table, or in the yard. Instead of asking open-ended questions, ask for simple but specific answers.

Eureka!

If you have carefully structured your line of questions, your child should end up right where you expected and chances are good that she will understand the steps of the concept better now that she has had to think through them logically. Additionally, as the child answers the questions, you can detect any misunderstandings and discuss them right away. Yes, it would be much easier to just tell them the answers, but then she wouldn't own her understanding, would she? Socratic Dialogue is an effective communication tool because the child learns to break the concept or idea up into components, organize the thoughts, and relate them to the parent. The conversation usually expands beyond the initial questions as a full-fledged discussion emerges, and your rising classical scholar practices the art of rhetoric through narration and Socratic Dialogue.

Chapter 27
Invention Reveals Truth for
Speeches and Essays

The oldest surviving Latin text on communicating effectively, *Rhetorica ad Herennium* (possibly written by the ancient Roman orator Cicero), outlines five canons or principles by which all rhetoric is judged. These five canons form a template for critiquing speeches and written compositions as well as a pattern for educating your home school children in rhetoric. Adopted from classical Greek rhetors (orators) like Isocrates, Plato, and Aristotle, this definitive guide to rhetoric was studied by the most famous orator in ancient Rome, Quintilian, as well as leading Christian medieval and Renaissance orators like Saint Augustine, Desiderius Erasmus, and Sir Francis Bacon.

Although our family has not read Cicero's original text, we use a contemporary text, *Classical Rhetoric for the Modern Student*, by Edward Corbett which extensively explains and illustrates this tradition that has been practiced in Western culture for over two thousand years. Over the next five chapters, I'll reveal the template or pattern of classical rhetoric. Canon one, INVENTION, is the subject of this chapter.

Determine the Topic

Discovering the main idea of the speech or essay is the first step of invention. What do you want to talk about in your speech or essay? Aristotle organized the potential topics of speeches into two categories: common and special. Common topics included definition of terms, division of the material into parts, comparison of similarities and contrast of differences, and testimonies of authorities. Common topics could be applied to any idea. Special topics were related to the three classical discourses and included justice, honor, and worthiness.

Sometimes we brainstorm for topics, but usually we simply select one of the more interesting subtopics of our home school academic reading (history, literature, philosophy, Scripture, science, etc). For example, Connor is reading about the battle of Gettysburg in the novel, *The Killer Angels*, by Michael Shaara. When I gave him the book to read, I told him that I wanted a ten paragraph paper from him on one debatable point. As he's read the compelling narrative, he's been struck by the honorable character of three officers: Lee, Longstreet, and Chamberlain. Now if you were heavily influenced by the stories your great grandmother told, you may not find all three men honorable because two of the men he's chosen to write about were Confederate officers and one a Union officer. However, Connor is going to argue that their characters transcended their national loyalties. That's a debatable point or idea; it's not a simple declaration of objective fact, but rather, whether his subjective conclusion is supported by evidence.

Discover the Arguments

During invention, ask lots of questions and discover arguments to support your point of view or case. In this exercise, try to find the core conflict of the debate. What is the real issue? Ancient orators asked four types of questions:

1. Is it true?

Questions of fact deal with truth which can be supported by actual objective evidence. In the example above, there are many facts to be examined such as Robert E. Lee and James Longstreet were both Confederate Generals while Joshua Chamberlain was a Union General.

2. What is it?

Questions of definition make a call about the nature of the idea. In our example, Connor would define character, the Confederacy, and the United States among other terms.

3. Is it important?

Questions of quality ask why the idea is important. Value judgments enter into these questions as each author will have differing opinions as to the importance or meaning of the idea.

4. Is this the right audience?

Questions of jurisdiction ask whether the venue for the speech or paper is the best for this issue or idea. An ancient orator would not present a deliberative speech to a judge just as the same orator would not present a forensic speech to a city council member.

The ultimate purpose of questions is to find arguments and evidence that support your point of view or case.

Develop the Thesis Statement

Once you've determined the topic of your speech or essay and developed the questions that support the topic, it's time to develop a thesis statement. The word thesis often gives my writing students the quakes, probably because a good thesis statement is generally more difficult to create than a topic sentence. A topic sentence is a declarative statement which states a general fact usually followed by supporting facts. A thesis statement is a debatable point or claim. To be debatable, there must be differing opinions or conflicting facts which call into question the validity of the statement. Thus, the orator or author must prove his idea or claim with hard evidence. To distinguish between a topic sentence and thesis statement, I'll provide an easy example from Connor's essay:

> Robert E. Lee, James Longstreet, and Joshua Chamberlain were men of character. (A topic sentence)

> Robert E. Lee, James Longstreet, and Joshua Chamberlain were men of character *because* they allowed their decent, chivalric upbringing to transcend their nationalistic loyalties. (A thesis statement)

What's the difference? The second sentence takes a position on each man's upbringing that must be proven with evidence whereas the first sentence is a statement of fact which does not claim to know why they were men of character. There could be many unique reasons for why each man has character which makes the idea debatable. The debatable component of the idea is what makes invention so much fun and challenging. We think to uncover the truth which is the essential purpose of canon one of classical rhetoric, invention. Once you've invented your debatable idea, you can move on to canon two, arrangement.

* * * * *

Do you have a child who struggles with writing thesis statements? Use the following acronym to help trigger debatable points: "www.asia." Although Andrew Pudewa teaches this as a stylistic dress up, I think you could use it for another purpose: developing a thesis. "www.asia" stands for:

when
while
where
as
since
if
although

If you tacked any of these words onto the end of a regular topic sentence then add a supporting phrase, you might have a thesis statement that needs proof. Try it next time!

Chapter 28
Teach the Art of Arrangement and Persuade Every Time

For the past three millennia, five principles or canons have governed the creation and execution of classical rhetoric. These five canons form a template for developing and critiquing speeches and written compositions. In canon one, invention, the orator or writer determines the topic, discovers the arguments, and develops the thesis for his speech or essay. Canon two, ARRANGEMENT, was called "dispositio" by the ancient Romans since it involved the disposition or arrangement of the idea and supporting arguments. Contemporary home school parents and even public school teachers spend an enormous amount of time teaching their students how to organize their thoughts often without consistent success. Let's take a look at how ancient, medieval, Renaissance, and colonial orators arranged their material.

Introduce the Idea

In the beginning of the speech or essay, the debatable idea was introduced. Ancient Romans called the introduction the exordium, and it was during this initial stage that the public speaker established his credibility and authority as an expert on the subject. Often the speaker referred to his knowledge or personal experience with the idea. Of course, the savvy orator selected evidence during the invention stage which highlighted his expertise so that the persuasive appeal of his personal character would lend weight to his arguments. Personal character, reputation, and intelligence were important factors in disposing the audience to listen and respond just as they are important to effective communication today.

Contemporary orators and writers often add a step before the introduction called the "attention-getter." Quotations, personal stories, jokes, or other compelling statistics open the speech so that the audience is immediately alert and receptive to the speech or essay.

State the Facts

The second part of a classical discourse was called narratio or narration. A narrative account of the facts is provided, and a general explanation of the case or idea is outlined. The current state of affairs or status quo was usually described with vivid word pictures that stirred the emotions and prepared the audience to consider the arguments favorably. Although a direct appeal to accept the arguments was not made at this point, the underlying intention of the narration was to move or persuade. Today, we call this portion of the speech or essay the exposition...the facts are exposed.

Outline the Proposal

Once the facts were stated and summarized, the ancient orator briefly outlined the evidence that was to follow. Contemporary audiences would recognize this ancient practice as the place in the speech where the speaker tells you what he's going to tell you! For example, after the attention-getter and introduction of the thesis statement, an excellent orator will "sign-post" where he's going with the speech or essay by using transition words like "first," "secondly," "next," "finally." Then he launches into the substance of the speech or essay.

Nail the Proof

Called the confirmation, this main body of the speech was devoted to the evidence. Quality content and logical arguments were imperative. It was here that the orator proved the points of his case or debatable idea. Now he would reveal the evidence that was derived during the question portion of the invention stage starting with the least powerful proof and gradually building to the most powerful and convincing proof as the climax of the argument.

The ancient orator used persuasive techniques like appeals to exhort the audience to recognize the benefits that would accrue to each of them if they adopted his position. He often appealed to material, spiritual, or emotional self-interest. (Contemporary copywriters call this technique "what's in it for me?") Sometimes, the orator exposed the inherent danger of acting on the opposing idea. Ethical and logical appeals were also made when the orator wanted to move the audience toward decisions of public good like caring for widows and orphans. Above all, the ancient orator appealed to reason or the logic of his case, so it's not surprising that ancient orators and audiences highly regarded critical thinkers.

The Third Road: Speech

Refute the Opposition

This portion of the speech was devoted to answering the counterarguments of one's opponents. Of course, in order to refute, the orator had to know both sides of the argument. During the invention stage, he gathered evidence for his case and against his case. Often during the speech, the orator asked imaginary questions in anticipation of the objections being raised in the minds of his audience; he then answered these imaginary objections. Sometimes the orator denigrated the authority or credibility of an opponent. At other times, the ancient orator found it useful to reject an alternative idea as immaterial, ridiculous, unnecessary, absurd, false, or morally wrong. Today we regularly reject opposing ideas as too expensive in terms of time and money.

Conclude and Call to Action

The peroration or conclusion of the speech included a summary of the debatable idea, the arguments, and the refutation in a compelling, climactic manner. The Greek word for climax means ladder and a rhetorical climax looks just like a ladder: the words, phrases, and ideas are arranged in a manner of increasing importance often in parallel structure. Usually, a final appeal was made to the listener to act on the orator's advice.

The Apostle Paul, trained in classical rhetoric, concludes the argument of chapter four and five of *The Epistle to the Romans* with a climactic conclusion:

> "We also boast in our *sufferings*, knowing that *suffering* produces *endurance*, and *endurance* produces *character*, and *character* produces *hope*, and *hope* does not disappoint us, because God's love has been poured into our hearts through the Holy Spirit that has been given to us." (Romans 5:3-5 NRSV)

Another example from Scripture of a classical conclusion is found in the genealogy of Jesus the Messiah at the beginning of Matthew, chapter one. After listing all the generations from Abraham to Jesus, Matthew concludes with:

> "So all the generations from Abraham to David are fourteen generations; and from David to the deportation to Babylon, fourteen generations; and from the deportation to

Babylon to the Messiah, fourteen generations." (Matthew 1:17 NRSV)

Arguably, the most famous peroration in Scripture could be the destruction of the Northern Kingdom, Israel, found in 2 Kings 17:1-22 which concludes the historian's exposition and arguments for the fall of Israel.

So now I hope you see how important artful arrangement is to the effective communication of the message and the ultimate persuasion of your audience. The orator or writer needs an introduction, a statement of facts, an outline, the proof, the refutation, and the conclusion. Although I've just given you a lot of detail, you can really boil classical rhetoric down to the idea, the proof, and the call to action.

* * * * *

One of the first exercises for teaching classical rhetoric in Quintilian's *Progymnasmata* was storytelling. If you have younger kids, prepare them for classical rhetoric now by teaching them how to narrate stories. Read them a story, close the book, and ask them to tell you the story in their own words. If they are having trouble, coach them through the beginning, middle, and end. Teach them how to ask the standard questions: who, what, when, where, how, and why. Eventually, they will learn how to quickly summarize the story which will be useful later when incorporating narratives in their speeches and writing as well as in literary analysis.

Chapter 29
Style: Painting Pictures with Words

The five canons or principles of classical rhetoric form a template for developing and critiquing speeches and written compositions. In canon one, invention, the orator or writer determines the debatable idea, discovers the logical arguments, and develops the thesis for his speech or essay. Canon two, arrangement, divides the speech or essay into the following parts: an introduction, a statement of facts, an outline, the proof, the refutation, and the conclusion. The third canon, STYLE, was known as elocutio (from loqui "to speak"), and of the five canons, style is the most difficult to define since each orator or writer expresses a unique creative energy. Breathtaking style is one of those nebulous things that is challenging to describe, but you know it when you see it! If invention is what you say, and arrangement is how you organize what you say, then style is how you say it.

What is your Purpose?

Ancient orators defined three levels of style: (1) low or plain, (2) middle or forcible, and (3) high or florid. In preparing the speech, the orator first decided his purpose. Was he going to instruct in the debatable idea? If so, he chose to use the low or plain style with his apprentices or students. His relationship with these individuals was more intimate so he had no need to impress them with sophisticated language or creative pleas. The instructional speech was more like a conversation in that practical information was passed along using normal, everyday language.

Perhaps the orator wanted to persuade an audience to act for the public good or judge a defendant as in political or legal speeches. In that case, he would choose the middle or forcible style of communication. An orator delivering a persuasive speech would probably speak to a larger audience which would have included many members whom he did not personally know or some who may have been enemies. The language for such an audience and purpose would be particular to the specific points of the debatable idea. Urging the audience to adopt his position, the skilled orator would choose convincing words and figures of speech such as metaphors and similes to coax his audience to his point of view.

Finally, many ceremonial occasions demanded oratory. Public holidays, religious festivals, weddings, funerals, and graduations require a lighter touch than the persuasive speech. Themes such as honor, patriotism, and faithfulness might be expounded. For such events, the orator would choose language to charm and entertain.

How Will you Arrange the Words?

Which words will you select? The choice of and arrangement of words in ancient times depended on the purpose of the speech and the audience to whom the speech was directed. Anyone who puts so much time and effort into preparing a speech or essay cares immensely about the appropriateness of the words because words have the power to move people.

Have you chosen the most appropriate words? Should they be pure and simple or ornate? Is specialized vocabulary needed? Does the grammar appear proper? Are the tenses consistent? Should you use the standard syntax for arranging the words or break a rule to produce an unexpected surprise? Would repetition of words or phrases be effective? Are your points concise? Have you chosen words that emotionally move the audience? Did you consider the sound and rhythm of the words and phrases? Would figures of speech like metaphor, personification, or simile aid in communicating your message?

William Strunk, Jr. and E.B. White, authors of *The Elements of Style*, say that style is a high mystery.

> "Who can confidently say what ignites a certain combination of words, causing them to explode in the mind?"

Each person approaches the same content differently; each of your children will manifest a unique style of speaking and writing that reveals something of his or her spirit. There are boundless opportunities for creative expression. Encourage your children to experiment with style as if they were painting pictures with words and delight their audience!

* * * * *

Here's a fun exercise. Take a much-quoted sentence, and have the kids play with rearranging the words. Stunk and White offer this example to get you started: "These are the times that try men's souls." Variations include:

1. Times like these try men's souls.
2. How trying it is to live in these times!
3. These are trying times for men's souls.
4. Soul wise, these are trying times.

Which sentence do you like best? Now it's your turn!

Chapter 30
Memory Is the Treasury of Invention

Canon four of classical rhetoric, MEMORY, involved the ability to recall the elements of the speech. Every great orator was expected to recite his speech from memory, but canon four was more than simply memorizing a speech. One author, perhaps Cicero, called memory the "treasury of things invented" meaning that memory was the place where all the components of the debatable idea were stored. Additionally, memory had to do with structuring the speech so that the audience would retain the content, too, through use of enumeration and vivid descriptions. Here are two memory techniques that I have found helpful in our classical home school.

See, Say, Hear, Write, Move

Once you've written the speech, it's time to start memorizing. Partition the speech into natural divisions (actors call these "beats" of character motivation), and tackle one section at a time. You could start with the introduction and learn each subsequent paragraph, or you might want to start with the conclusion and work your way backward to the beginning of the speech. Both methods work.

When you select a segment to memorize, start by reading the entire section out loud. Not only are your eyes storing the content, but your ears are storing the data, too. Experiment with pronunciation, intonation, and pacing as you read the text. Decide which words or phrases are important enough to punctuate verbally with pauses, rising volume, or crisp consonants. Carefully listen to yourself speak. After you've read through this section, copy the text word for word, reading aloud as you write.

Now stand up and go back to the first sentence. Read it aloud while moving until you can recite it from memory. You might try an outstretched arm at an appropriate moment, or you might walk to the right and place your hands on your hips. Do the same with the second sentence, and this time, recite sentences one and two. Add sentence three so that now you recite the first three sentences from memory. Continue this repetitive layering technique until you've got the entire paragraph memorized. When you've got the first paragraph memorized, start on paragraph number two. Follow the same procedure and recite both paragraphs from memory. Keep plugging away by using all your senses until you've got the whole speech down.

Imagine the Room

Ancient orators used to "place" certain portions of the speech in the room where they would give the speech. For instance, if Quintilian was preparing a speech for his students gathering in the Roman Forum, he might go to the Forum and walk around looking for distinct images which he could then tag as he memorized his speech. He decided in advance where he would physically deliver or geographically "place" each component of the speech: the intro to the center steps, point number one to the marble column on the left, point number two to the statuary on the right, and the conclusion to the entrance. As the speech unfolds, each section is recalled as the images are viewed. This technique involves tagging by association; when you want to recall a certain portion of the speech, think of the tag, and you'll remember the content associated with that tag.

So what do you do when you aren't able to visualize or visit the room in advance? Use a room from your home for tagging the speech. Place point one at the sofa, point two at the coffee table, and the conclusion at the piano. Or you might want to use a familiar traveling route as your tags...from the garage to the mailbox to the entrance to the subdivision to the traffic light to the grocery store. Do you see how this works? Learning experts say that your brain forms associations between your environment and circumstances. An example of this is the bombing of the World Trade Center; you probably remember exactly where you were and what you were doing when you heard the tragic news even though it's been years since the event. Your brain uses spatial and otherwise meaningful clues to store and retrieve information.

* * * * *

Our brains have an amazing capacity to memorize large portions of scripts and speeches. As a speech coach and frequent judge at NCFCA speech and debate tournaments, I always prefer a memorized speech over a script that is read word for word. The student who commits the speech or debate constructive to memory is free to make eye contact, tailor the text to the needs of the audience, and receive nonverbal feedback as a result. These two techniques are not limited to formal speeches given by teens. Use these two techniques now to help younger children memorize short poems, Bible passages, and even foreign languages. If your younger child is not yet reading, you can read the poem or passage into a cassette recorder or mp3 player for the "hear it" portion of the memory technique. Start now and watch your child's "treasury of invention" grow!

Chapter 31
Voice and Gestures Personalize Speech Delivery

DELIVERY, classical rhetoric canon number five, is like style in that it determines how something is said. The Greek word for delivery, hypokrisis, translates in English as "acting," so it's not surprising that canon five focuses on vocal training and the use of gestures. Writers must make up for the lack of physical delivery in brilliant style.

Effective Use of Voice

You've probably heard the legend of the Athenian orator, Demosthenes, who, in order to overcome a severe stutter, purportedly ran along the Greek seashore reciting poetry with pebbles in his mouth. His efforts paid off in the long run as he became an eloquent public speaker. These days the only people who seriously study vocal techniques are singers, actors, and some elite politicians. Singers and actors know that the proper use of the diaphragm results in more oxygen which leads to more volume and pitch control. Likewise, an open larynx and dropped jaw allow the sound to resonate creating a clearer tone as the notes vibrate against the bones of the head. The deliberate rhetor articulates vowels, consonants, and diphthongs for accurate, crisp pronunciation.

An experienced orator often plays with vocal techniques before settling on the final spoken piece. When still preparing the presentation, he experiments with the following elements:

- pitch (the musical tone on a standard scale like the note "middle C")
- volume (the loudness or softness of sounds)
- pause (the temporary suspension of sound)
- emphasis (the stress placed on certain sounds, words, or phrases)
- rhythm (the ordered alternation between strong and weak elements)
- pace (the speed at which the words are spoken)
- tone (the mood or intensity of the spoken words)

100

Consider that a speech is somewhat like a personalized work of art. Each orator will bring unique vocal attributes to the very same text. Use your voice to decorate the content.

Effective Use of Gestures

Now it's time to involve the entire body as an instrument of communication. Plan your physical movement from your head down to your toes. Will you nod your head up and down at key points? Perhaps you will tilt it in a certain manner. Generally, your arms should relax comfortably at your side with fists unclenched unless you are using your arms and hands for specific illustrations. Don't point your fingers unless you want to threaten your audience. Decisions need to be made about your legs as well. Will you walk to certain points during the speech to accentuate specific points in the content? Will you adopt a stable stance of good posture for most of the speech? How will you manage your eyes and face? Eye contact is critical, but don't flit from person to person. Engage certain members of the audience with a direct gaze. Consider the overall theme or message that you want to communicate and make sure that your physical delivery is consistent with that message. A ceremonial speech might use a greater variety of casual gestures where a deliberative speech might use less gestures of a more formal nature.

* * * * *

One of the best ways to investigate vocal and physical delivery options is to observe other excellent public speakers! Pay attention to the techniques used by political candidates, actors, and soloists, and imitate their best ideas in your next speech. Above all, practice makes perfect, as the old saying goes!

Chapter 32
The Audience Is Always Right

Successful home school communicators consider the audience who will read or hear the composition before they begin researching the topic. Think about how a speech on euthanasia might be received by each of these audiences:

- a few medical doctors who work at the local hospice
- a Sunday School class of 11 and 12 year old girls
- a funeral home director and his staff
- a group of state or federal legislators
- a gathering of elderly nursing home residents
- a convention of pharmaceutical reps

Obviously, each of these collective audiences would have a different perspective and perhaps a biased self-interest in advocating or outlawing euthanasia. No two audiences are ever the same. (My speech students who compete in different regions of the country know this hard fact!) Excellent public speakers do their best to assess the audience in advance and tailor the message accordingly. If poor or unenlightened choices are made during the content phase, the message may be doomed no matter how brilliant the delivery. Failure to communicate ultimately rests with the speaker because the audience is always right.

Whether addressing a parent, a small group of friends, a few thousand newsletter subscribers, or an auditorium full of paid attendees, the public speaker and writer is particularly challenged by this compound question:

Who is my audience, and how will I reach them?

Understanding the audience - who they are, how they think and feel, and what they need - is essential to effective communication. This concept applies to all ages and levels of expertise: from the little boy who desperately wants another cookie to the grandparent who needs a ride to the pharmacy to the teenage debater who hopes to persuade the judge to vote affirmative. Possible attitudes toward your appeal include:

- supportive (they agree with you)
- apathetic (they don't care)
- doubtful (they're not sure or have serious reservations)
- hostile (they are actively opposed)
- knowledgeable (they already know a great deal)
- unlearned (they know nothing about it)
- indifferent (the thought never occurred to them)

Knowing some key facts about the audience favorably impacts the message. The speech or essay can then be crafted in such a way that the ideas have personal meaning and relevance to your unique audience. People pay attention to ideas that compliment their own hopes, needs, and goals.

Savvy public speakers and writers adjust the theme (invention), structure (arrangement), style, vocabulary, length, and delivery to each audience. If addressing a large, heterogeneous audience, more explicit syntax and background information is needed. If addressing a specialized niche (for instance, baseball players), specialized language (like earned run averages) can be used to illuminate. What do the members of the audience have in common? Do you expect them to be good listeners? Can you estimate collective age, social status, ethnicity, education, and cultural background? Consult others who have spoken before similar audiences in the past, or check out any written records (bylaws, public minutes) that are available about the group. Will the surroundings such as lighting, acoustics, and distance impact their ability to favorably respond to you?

Communication is an exchange of information. The word exchange implies giving and taking. The orator or writer gives three things: (1) a debatable idea, (2) the evidentiary proof, and (3) a call to action. The audience receives this offering and responds with verbal, nonverbal, and sometimes written feedback. Nothing is more deflating and discouraging to a home school public speaker or writer than a tepid, unresponsive audience. To improve immediate feedback, consider adding novelty, humor, contrast, movement, suspense, and intensity to command attention. Above all, tailor the message to the audience. Certainly, the audience has the right to disagree as in the case of the mom who refuses the second cookie, but if the audience doesn't understand the idea, plea, argument, or information, somehow the author has failed to communicate. Although it's hard work, effective communication rests primarily with the creator of the message because the audience is always right!

The Destination

&

Mastery

Chapter 33
Gentlemen, Start Your Engines!

Every May, nearly 300,000 people gather in Indianapolis, Indiana for the "world's greatest racing spectacle," an exciting 200 lap, 500 mile race. Adrenaline rushes as the cars fly around the track, traveling the length of a football field in one second, at speeds exceeding 220 mph. The sleek fiberglass shell of the Indy car hides a powerful engine that can run at 675 horsepower which is four times that of an average car. As drivers compete for placement in the turns, they endure G-force of four times the weight of gravity which is comparable to the G-force of the space shuttle take offs. Experienced pit crews perform mechanical magic as they refuel and replace worn tires in an astounding 20 seconds or less. Aggressive, careless, or tired drivers occasionally lose control of their cars, and the yellow caution flags come out when fiery crashes bring the manic race to a screeching halt. Finally, after three exhilarating and exhausting hours, the checkered flag appears, and the victory celebration begins!

Content :: Laps

In an Indy 500 race, the driver completes 200 circuits around the race track. Each time that he completes a lap, he accumulates knowledge like how well the car is running, the condition of the track, and which competitors are advancing. In addition to his own observations, he maintains constant radio contact with the crew chief who warns him of impending dangers and counsels him to push harder. Over the course of time, he gains more and more practical experience to support his theoretical knowledge about racing.

Think of the three skills of the trivium like laps in a race track. In the beginning of the race, your child knows nothing about reading, thinking, and speaking. With patient persistence and a good plan, you begin to coach them through the laps until they are moving faster and becoming proficient in language, thought, and speech abilities. The content of your instruction is like a lap. One day you might decide to teach a lap in grammar skills, or perhaps you run several laps of various content from all three skills. Use the road maps for mastery of reading, thinking, and speaking skills to plan your particular race.

Each family will teach content differently. Let's take an example. Learning how to research and develop arguments are two components of critical thinking. These skills can be taught in various ways. For instance, my husband, David, is an attorney who sometimes finds himself before a federal judge. Learning how to research and debate a national or international resolution meets my husband's criteria for teaching research skills, developing an argument, listening well, and giving a speech. Consequently, participation in our local debate club is mandatory for the Lockman kids! Whereas, your husband may be an engineer who believes research is best learned in a lab setting and communicated in a research paper. Tailor the content and methods to best meet your family's abilities and preferences.

Child :: Driver

Some glamorous Indy Car celebrities grew up in renowned racing families, but no matter how famous Daddy was, junior didn't inherit all the skill necessary for racing success through raw DNA replication. All champions have to learn the basic rules of driving just like every other licensed driver. Once the basics are mastered, the beginner can move on to more sophisticated concepts. Your child is no different. Every master began as a novice.

Mastery of the three skills is not consecutive; the skills are usually built concurrently over time. In other words, your child doesn't master language then master critical thinking then master public speaking. In fact, your child can work on mastering all three skills at the same time. Consider the child who is learning about multiplication. As he learns vocabulary words like factor and product (language), he makes ordered stacks with the colored manipulative tiles (thought) and sings the multiplication songs to his little brother (speech).

Additionally, you may find that your child has substantially mastered one skill (like the spelling component of language) but is still working on another skill set (the grammar component of language). Instead of drilling the spelling rules, devote that time to diagramming sentences.

Parents :: Pit Crew

The highly-skilled mechanics who work on Indy Car crews are some of the best in the world. They receive regular training as technology advances. They know their cars and drivers so well that they can anticipate problems and solutions before they crop up. Quick to respond, they are proactive, monitoring the status of the vehicle with wireless radio and detailed gauge readings. To give your kids an authentic classical home education, you need to be current on all that you are teaching. Plan time to refresh your memory if you are a little rusty (call it "Mom's continuing education"), or do a little advance reading before you need to teach a concept. You'll be more confident and serve your children's needs better if you are prepared. If you find yourself unprepared, that's okay, too. Declare a reading week and catch up! The kids will love the break!

Indy Cars enter the pit for one reason: maintenance. Periodically throughout the race, the driver pulls into the pit for fuel, tire changes, and for other engine or body work. The experienced pit crew member assesses the situation and prescribes a solution. Personally, we like regular pit stops in our home! I reassess the kids' progress at least once a semester using my road maps to mastery, and then I adjust the schedule and content accordingly. Weaker areas get more time. Sometimes I'll even table all other work and do a quick blitz to make sure they thoroughly understand the concept. We've been known to stop everything and do an "intensive camp" until I was satisfied that they "got it." Be flexible, and perform regular maintenance.

Grades :: Points

Indy Car drivers accumulate points over the racing season as they compete in multiple races around the country. You need criteria for judging mastery, too. How will you evaluate learning?

In our home, we have one performance philosophy: do it well, or do it over. We don't accept mediocrity. Once Connor lost control of his "car," and I had to start waving the caution flag and call the referee. Performing poorly on his math lessons, he was consistently scoring in the 60-70% range. As experienced pit chief, I suspected that the problem had to do with a lack of discipline more than a lack of understanding. My husband took control of the situation and started grading Connor's work. Instead of circling the errors, he simply told our son how many problems he missed. Connor was responsible for finding the errors. Since Daddy didn't circle the incorrect answers, Connor had to do every problem again. Although it was a painful lesson, Connor learned to take his time, check his work, and master the material.

Personally, I think keeping track of grades in the early years is pure busy work. Unless your state board of education requires it, I would not bother. The task of grading and recording results is so time consuming, and it reduces available teaching time; however, my kids are both going to college, so I need to comply with the generally accepted admission requirements and produce a GPA for the transcript. I'll cover grades in detail in my next book on the post-trivium years. More importantly, I evaluate mastery using a scale that I found in John Milton Gregory's book, *The Seven Laws of Teaching*. Each semester, I examine the skills and decide how much my child knows about each one. For instance, how much does he know about punctuation?

1. He knows nothing about…
2. He is somewhat familiar with…
3. He can generally describe the steps to…
4. He can illustrate and explain how to…
5. He is beginning to understand the deeper truths of…
6. He is changing his behavior because of…

When your child reaches the "changing behavior" status, you know that he has mastered the material. The child who can draft a paper with perfect punctuation has mastered the ability to punctuate. Realistically, though, no human will ever absolutely master each skill, so look for substantial mastery before declaring that teaching task complete. Substantial is defined as sizeable or significant; therefore, the child who only occasionally makes punctuation errors has substantially mastered the ability to punctuate, and you can establish a new goal.

Finally, I use another assessment tool to determine whether my kids have mastered the material: teaching others. You cannot teach what you do not know, and there is nothing like having to prepare a lesson that clarifies your misunderstandings or weaknesses. By the way, the word "master" is defined as "one who has such extensive knowledge and comprehensive skill that he is able to teach others his specialty."

Trivium Mastery :: Finish Line

Extreme speed may be a characteristic of the Indy 500, but trivium mastery requires a slower pace. Unlike the race which only takes three hours, your journey will take years of training, repetition, and application. Expect to spend at least six to eight years exclusively teaching the three skills of the classical trivium, but don't get discouraged if it takes longer. As you will discover in Part Two, Twelve Classical Makeovers, each child is unique and requires a tailored plan. Additionally, some skills will be mastered long before others, and depending on your family's preferred content, other tasks will be intentionally omitted.

The leader of the Indy 500 Race clearly sees the checkered flag when he makes the final turn of lap 200. When he crosses the finish line, he knows without a doubt, that he is done. Your task is a little more ambiguous. The first several years of classical home schooling are spent teaching three skills until substantial mastery. You know that your child has reached the finish line when he has consummate possession of language, thought, and speech.

Practically, your son or daughter needs to have such command of the English language that the vocabulary, complex sentence structure, and literary style of the classics are not overwhelming. The ability to comprehend and wrestle with the meaning of the written text is also necessary. Finally, the young adult who is ready to move on has the skill to write extensively about abstract concepts like redemption, freedom, and peace.

Chapter 34
Are We There Yet?

We live more than 600 miles from our family. Trips home to visit are grueling contests of endurance. When the kids were younger, a plaintive cry from the back seat never failed to materialize:

"Are We There Yet?"

Inevitably, the answer was no with an explanation of how much longer we had to go. Long journeys require physical, mental, and spiritual strength. They are not easy. If mastery of the three skills (language, thought, and speech) is the ultimate goal of the early years of authentic classical home schooling, how will you know when you have arrived at your destination?

Most people prepare for long distance trips by consulting maps. Let's say that you are going on a two week vacation to explore a chain of U. S. National Parks. Together, you and your spouse decide on which parks you want to visit. Then you have to look at the distance between parks and decide upon the order of your trip. Armed with a tentative itinerary, you use the scale on the map to determine how many miles you'll have to cover each day so that you can make appropriate lodge or campground reservations. If you are like me, you make a "to-do" list to make sure you don't forget any critical action steps like sending deposits.

Next, you might purchase a travel guide or go to the library to learn more about the activities offered at the selected parks. More reservations for guided tours, burro rides, or white water rafting excursions follow. As the trip draws closer, you complete the final preparations like packing suitcases, delivering pets to the kennel, withdrawing cash from the bank, and filling the gasoline tank. When departure day arrives, you load the car, and off you go on an exciting adventure!

Inevitably, a crisis will interrupt the perfect plans of the trip. A child gets sick, a tire blows, or perhaps the state highway patrol has created a detour that takes you off of your planned path. What do you do? You adapt. You pull off and purchase some medicine. You replace the tire. You consult the map again for a new route.

Teaching the three skills of the classical trivium is like taking an extended road trip. You wouldn't hop in the car and head west without a plan, would you? Of course not! You need a plan for the trivium journey, too. Here are five concrete steps to guarantee rewarding travel.

1. Appraise

Whether you have a six year old or a thirteen year old, you need to establish a baseline for mastery. List every subject being studied. This will help you later when you have to decide what to eliminate and what to add. After you have done this, take the *Road Map for Mastery of Reading Skills* (chapter 7) and mentally estimate how far along your child is towards mastery. Confirm or refute your expectations by sitting down with each child and assessing mastery step by step. For instance, when deciding if your child has mastered the language skill, "how to use proper grammar," have him identify the eight parts of speech from a passage in the book he is currently reading.

Start at the beginning. Has he mastered reading? Check that task off, and move on to spelling. Is he still struggling with consistent application of some spelling rules? Leave that task unchecked, make a note of his weakness, and move on. Stop evaluating when the child struggles with a concept, and move on to the next skill. Completion of the road map shouldn't take more than 30 minutes to an hour. You inherently know what areas need work.

After you've evaluated language skills, pull out the *Road Map for Mastery of Thinking Skills* (chapter 13), and repeat the process. Finally, evaluate mastery of speaking skills with the road map in chapter 21. Now you've got your baseline for establishing a written plan.

2. Reflect

Complete the interview questions which are found in the appendix of this book. This may seem like an unnecessary step, but you need to know who you are as a family and what themes define you so that you can tailor the plan.

Write all of your answers down on paper, or type them so that you can print a copy for later consultation. Once you have completed the questionnaire, spend some quiet time reflecting on how you would describe your family. Try to briefly summarize who you are as a family unit from the past to the present. Certain themes will surface. Ask yourself: what are the recurring themes of our family's story? Write a short narrative that would succinctly tell a stranger who you are as a family. This exercise is important because it highlights the strengths and values of the parents which will help you direct your joint teaching efforts.

3. Plan

Create a one page summary of the skills that your child needs to work on this semester. Here's an example:

READING SKILLS

How to punctuate and capitalize

THINKING SKILLS

How to solve problems
How to structure and analyze arguments
How to analyze literature

SPEAKING SKILLS

How to write a paragraph
How to give a speech

Now that you have an idea of what skills he has mastered and what skills still need work, draft concrete action steps for the semester. Eliminate all work in areas that he has already mastered. Did you discover that he was unfamiliar with gerunds and participles? Incorporate some time in the plan for learning these concepts. Are footnotes a problem? Include practice footnoting authorities in his next essay or research paper. Don't try to cover everything in the first semester.

Finally, create a to-do list for yourself and your children. Include materials that you need to purchase as well as concepts that you need to brush up on. Share your findings with your spouse and divide the work according to ability, interest, and available time.

4. Execute

Once you have gathered all of your supplies and checked off all your todos, carry out your plan. Have fun!

5. Adjust

After a few weeks, pull out your road map, the semester plan, and assess progress. Cut out any steps that didn't achieve your objectives, and add new action steps accordingly. You don't have to rewrite the original document each time. If you don't have the time or are more comfortable with bullet points, by all means, do what works for your family.

Every now and then, remind yourself that you are giving your child the inheritance that you never had as a child: an authentic classical education which will prepare him to be a thinker and leader. Can you believe it? You are raising a classical scholar! Your children are reclaiming the inheritance that you never received. Remember that mastery of the three skills is a process that takes time. Eventually, you will experience the extreme satisfaction of watching your child reach the intersection of the three roads of the classical trivium. When he asks, "Mom, are we there yet?" you can finally say, "yes, we've made it, son!" Well done, friend! Well done.

Chapter 35
The Next Journey: The Pursuit of Knowledge

While celebration is appropriate, mastery of the three skills is not achieved on a single day in history. You will never be able to look back and pinpoint a day as "the day when your child arrived." Some time during the teen years, you will realize that he has become extremely proficient in the use of language, thought, and speech. There could be some areas of the trivium that he still needs to work on, but by and large, he is ready for more. For what has the classical trivium prepared him?

The Roman Quadrivium

If this were ancient Rome, your rising scholar would progress to the remaining four liberal arts of the the quadrivium taught by a private tutor: arithmetic, geometry, astronomy, and music theory. The pragmatic Romans took the Greek idea of paideia and decided that every free man should learn seven "arts" in order to be fully educated. Nearly three millennia later, we know that learning the four mathematically-oriented disciplines of the quadrivium is no longer sufficient. Unlike the timeless skills of the trivium, the Roman quadrivium is obsolete.

A staggering amount of discoveries have been made since then in math, science, and technology that preclude any man from being a true expert. The inherited body of knowledge accumulates at a frenzied pace as the record of human history continues. In short, the choices for learning in the 21st Century are limitless. Yet, there still remains a core set of fundamental truths with which every educated man and woman should grapple.

The Greek Paideia

You may recall that the Greek paideia is the foundation of a true classical education. According to *Webster's Third New International Dictionary*, paideia is the:

> "Training of the physical and mental facilities in such a way as to produce a broad enlightened mature outlook harmoniously combined with maximum cultural development."

Learning was the path to a higher nature through the exploration of abstract concepts such as truth, goodness, and beauty with the expectation that such examination would lead to noble character, gracious behavior, enlightened minds, and enriched society. However, the early Greek culture from which classical education arose was pagan, and as Emperor Charlemagne realized hundreds of years later, classical education would never accomplish its true objectives unless informed by relationship with the Living God. Man is limited in his knowledge. He needs inspiration. The Greek paideia is not enough.

The Christian Paideia

Most contemporary Christians cannot read Koine Greek, the language of the *New Testament*, unless they have been to seminary, so you might be surprised to discover that the Apostle Paul uses the word paideia at least seven times in the *New Testament* in his letters to the Hebrews, the Ephesians, and to his disciple Timothy. Upon reflection, this isn't really surprising because as I discussed in the chapters on rhetoric, there is quite a bit of textual evidence that Paul received a classical education with a concentration in Jewish theology.

I believe we can take the Greek idea of paideia (the search for knowledge) and look at Paul's use of the word paideia (discipline or instruction in righteousness) to understand the next journey for our kids. True education is a transformational process of growing in knowledge, understanding, and wisdom.

In the early section of the first letter to the Corinthians, Paul spends a lot of time developing the thought that God's foolishness is wiser than man's wisdom. God reveals His knowledge to those who love Him so that they can worship and serve Him in spirit and truth. Unlike the unrealized dreams of the ancient Greeks, our search for knowledge is exquisitely fulfilling as the Lord of Glory reveals little bits of truth in our daily walk with His abiding Spirit. Faithful followers use what they have learned in service to others. Enlightenment for the sake of service is our final objective. In this way, we reclaim our classical inheritance and join the long line of ancestors who realized the wealth of a true classical education.

Dialogue Drives Instruction

So what does this look like for teens who have substantially mastered the three skills of the classical trivium? To adequately answer that question, another book is required! In the meantime, here are a few key characteristics of the post-trivium years:

- Socratic conversations
- Independent study
- Source documents
- Western classics
- Extensive writing
- Apprenticeships
- Cross cultural travel
- Community Service
- Leadership opportunities

This "socratic paideia" looks vastly different from the traditional public school paradigm for high school, yet there is a tension between the application of these characteristics and the accumulation of information for an acceptable transcript for college admission. When you feel that your kids are approaching mastery, you can read all about the post-trivium years in the imminent sequel to this book, *Socratic Paideia: Dialogue Drives Instruction*. In the meantime, enjoy the years of the trivium, and recover from the urban legend that has hijacked the classical Christian home schooling renewal movement! You can do it!

PART TWO

&

TWELVE CLASSICAL MAKEOVERS

Chapter 36
Case Study Methodology

Wrestling with the theoretical ideas of classical education has been a very satisfying experience, but I would consider all of this time and energy wasted effort if I were not able to translate that knowledge and understanding into practical everyday application that can be used by the average parent in the average home. Observation and interpretation are important to me, but I really enjoy taking an idea and applying it to real life. Deep down, I value pragmatism over idealism. In other words, if I can't make the ideals work in my own home, they are worthless. Likewise, if they don't work in your home, they are equally worthless.

But, every home is unique just as every child is unique. So, I decided instead of telling you how to apply the ideas of classical education in your own home, I would show you how to apply them by interviewing twelve children between the ages of five and thirteen.

In order to prove my theories, I asked five families to participate in case studies. The names of all the individuals have been changed to protect their identities. (In fact, each child picked a pseudonym or alternate identity.) Each mother completed a questionnaire about the members of the family and her educational philosophy. Once she finished telling me about herself, her spouse, her children, and her home schooling experience, we met (either in person or via telephone) for a more in-depth conversation.

After that, I interviewed each child in order to assess mastery of the three skills of the trivium. While chatting, I inquired about interests, abilities, and favorite pastimes. During the interview, I guided each child through all three "road maps for mastery" of reading, thinking, and speaking skills. I also selected certain tools, found in the appendix, to assess progress. Additionally, each family provided writing samples for me to examine. Next, I sequestered myself and wrote a strategic semester plan for each child, a to-do list for the parents, and a to-do list for the children.

Throughout the entire process, I prayed for wisdom and insight because I wanted to provide a customized plan for each child that uniquely met the needs of the parents and the child while illustrating for you, my reader, exactly what I am talking about when I say "teach the skills of the trivium to substantial mastery." Imagine that you are the parent, and I am writing directly to you with recommendations for traveling the three roads of mastery.

I hope that as you read each case study, you will begin to visualize the freedom of an authentic classical Christian home education. Each strategic semester plan is tailored to meet the dreams and needs of the individual while mastering the three skills of the trivium. After you have read through all twelve makeovers, set aside time to complete the questionnaire for your family and use my "road maps for mastery" along with selected tools from the appendix to pinpoint the areas of strengths and weaknesses for each of your children so that you can create a custom short-term plan that works, too.

First Family

&

John, Rebecca, Two Sons, and Two Daughters

Chapter 37
Eclectic Education

Education has been a theme for this family since the very beginning! John was a young business professor at the university where Rebecca was working on her undergraduate degree in psychology. Mutual friends arranged to accompany them on a blind date that soon led to marriage. Eighteen years later, four children, ranging in age from 7 to 17, a dog, a cat, and a rat round out the family.

John is a natural leader in the community and his home. Previously the Associate Dean of the business school, he recently scaled back his university responsibilities and went back to being a faculty member so that he would have more time with his family. His flexible schedule often allows him to come home early in the afternoons to help the kids with math or go on field trips. Not surprisingly, his communication skills are superior since he lectures college students and writes for technical journals on a regular basis. For the past eight years, he has taught the high school kids at his church, including his own teens, Scripture, Church History, and Theology. He also leads his family in evening Scripture readings.

Rebecca has a servant's heart. A faithful volunteer in her community, she has served senior citizens, women, and home school families in various leadership roles for a cumulative combined total of forty years! Her favorite subjects are reading and writing especially editing her husband's and children's papers. Her children all know a comma splice when they see one! The Barnes and Noble clearance department is one of her favorite haunts.

Rebecca describes herself as eclectic or independent in her approach to home schooling. She says, "I love choices!" Spend a few minutes getting to know her better by reading her responses to my questions about home schooling.

When were you first introduced to the idea of home schooling?

> The year before I started, I found out that two friends that I admired (both from out of town) were home schooling, so that opened my mind to considering it. I was already looking into anything but public school because I was feeling a spiritual "no" on sending my oldest son there when it was time.

Why did you decide to teach your kids at home?

Every time I talked to one of those two friends, I felt the Spirit bear witness to me that home schooling was a good thing, so I prayerfully researched all I could about it and soon realized it was the Lord's will for us. We combined faith with works, and we've never looked back!

How long have you been home schooling?

We are beginning the 11th year this fall.

What moments related to home schooling have brought you the greatest joy?

Just being beside my children each day, seeing them work through things and growing in their learning and understanding has brought me joy.

What moments related to home schooling have brought you the most frustration?

At times feeling unable to help my child's feelings of failure, searching for a math program that will work, seeing the children sometimes seem unwilling to put forth true effort, and dealing with my own laziness and inability to teach history effectively have been my greatest frustrations.

How organized would you say your home school is?

I would say we are moderately organized. Sunday night I write out the coming week's schedule for each child with each day's assignments on it and then they check off as each one is done. Overall, I'm not "long-term organized" though I have become more so with high school plans.

How structured is your typical day?

Our day is fairly structured. The kids get up around 7 a.m. After breakfast, they get their morning jobs done (by 8:15 a.m.) and read until 9 a.m. Then they "do school" until noon with a snack break around 10 a.m. After lunch, we resume school for another hour or two.

Do you take breaks throughout the calendar year?

We loosely follow the public school year in that we typically take a 2 to 3 week break over Christmas and New Year's Day and a spring break around (not necessarily at) the time other schools do. We begin our school year a few weeks later than public school (after Labor Day) and end a few weeks later in June, which maximizes the summertime and is more typical of the systems with which my husband and I grew up. If schools are off due to weather or in-service, we still have school unless there's lots of fun snow!

Do you have a dedicated room just for school?

No, we have a huge country kitchen with lots of sunlight, so the kitchen table serves as the school table, and nearby are two 6' bookshelves full of school materials. I LOVE sitting at the end of the table with my children on either side of me, teaching them, watching them, and helping as needed.

What general areas do you feel qualified to teach?

Grammar, art, cooking, and critical thinking

Are there any areas of study in which you feel inadequate?

Writing, math, science, and history

Are there other things that you want to teach them that you haven't had time to do yet?

I'd like to do more with art and have that tentatively factored into my schedule, but then I had it scheduled in all this past semester and rarely did it.

What is your biggest concern or question about giving your kids a classical education?

I'm concerned that I'm not fully utilizing a classical education, which is what I believe is the best form of education for my children, particularly if they're going to attend college where they will undoubtedly have demanding and challenging courses.

* * * * *

John and Rebecca's two oldest children, Ashlie (17) and Tim (14), are both pursuing high school level studies, and as such, their makeovers are included in the sequel to this book, *Socratic Paideia: Dialogue Drives Instruction.*

The makeovers for 11 year old son, Kenneth, and 7 year old daughter, Morgan, follow. I hope that you enjoy meeting them as much as I did!

Chapter 38
A Knack for Superb Impressions

Inquisitive is a good adjective to describe 11 year old Kenneth. He loves solving problems, and mystery board games like *Clue*, *Guess Who*, *Guess Where*, and *Scrambled States of America* are all favorite pastimes. He enjoys playing video games with his older brother of the racing (NASCAR and snowboarding) genre. Professional tennis, football, and basketball games also garner his attention; he is an avid fan of the Broncos and the Celtics. A natural athlete, Kenneth plays kickball, skates, and shoots hoops when he has the chance. Unlike most people, he has a knack for superb impressions which indicates he pays attention to precise details and has the potential to readily imitate the spoken and written word.

Mastery Status

Kenneth is well on his way to mastering the English language, the first skill set of the classical trivium. The only area of language that he needs to work on is his oral reading skills; other than that, the suggestions below relate more to improvement than to weaknesses. He is a thinker, so he will enjoy the challenge of playing logic games and tackling a more comprehensive math curriculum while traveling the second road, thought. Kenneth is just now encountering the third skill, speech, so now is the time to introduce the basics of excellent writing. Expect him to spend the bulk of his time on skills two and three over the next few years while he masters thinking and speaking skills.

Kenneth's semester priorities:

READING SKILLS

How to read
How to spell
How to punctuate and capitalize

THINKING SKILLS

How to arrange data according to systems
How to solve problems
How to analyze literature

SPEAKING SKILLS

How to write a paragraph
How to give a speech

Action Steps

1. Have him listen to one book a week and practice reading out loud.

Kenneth is reading very well, but his tone is relatively flat. Listening to advanced readers add feeling, pauses, and drama where appropriate will naturally teach him to do the same when he reads out loud. You have at least two options: you can read to him, or you can provide audio books. Explain to him that the people who record audio books are usually actors or radio talk show personalities who intentionally think about the way the text sounds. Conveying a mental picture that transports the reader is the objective.

Commit to a weekly library trip, and let him select books for practicing his own oral reading skills. Encourage him to pick easy picture books (under his ability) with dialogue for a weekly practice session with you. These are not the primary books that he will read; these are more like short scripts for practicing acting. Point out places where he could speak with more emotion, and make him do it over until he does it well.

If Morgan wants to get involved, Kenneth may want to select books with more than one character so that sister and brother can share the dialogue. One act plays might also be fun for them both; have them split up the parts and read aloud. Who knows? They might find one that they want to fine tune so that they can present it to the family.

2. Continue the abridged classics and comprehension questions.

He's a great reader for his age; he handled vocabulary of increasing difficulty in the sample reading excerpts. The only one that he had trouble with was the second hardest excerpt which was taken from the unabridged version of *Redwall*; he struggled with the pronunciation of three or four words.

He is spending quite a lot of time reading the abridged classics, so continue to encourage daily reading. Since he likes the prewritten comprehension questions, you can continue to assign them, but eventually you want to wean him off of the canned questions and have him ask his own questions. He said that handwriting sometimes causes cramps in his hands, so you might want to wait on having him write out his own questions.

3. Have a weekly spelling bee or play a game of Scrabble.

Kenneth's advanced vocabulary allows him to recognize words when he sees them, but can he spell them if he is asked to? He likes spelling, so hold a weekly spelling bee by selecting 10 or 15 words from his abridged classics and have him spell them. Provide a goodie for a job well done. Scrabble tiles are another option for checking spelling; just give him a word and ask him to assemble the letters correctly.

Additionally, you could dictate one quality paragraph a week from his abridged classic. Circle the spelling errors and have him correct them. If you see a pattern over time (one particular spelling or punctuation rule being broken), take time to teach him the proper rule and let him practice getting it right. For example, the rule "i before e, except after c" could be a problem; if so, give him some words to spell that follow this rule like "field, tried, and yield." Don't forget to quiz him on the exceptions, too.

4. Dictate one short paragraph a week to punctuate.

Discontinue formal grammar work. He knows all eight parts of speech as well as the four sentence structures. If you feel like he needs a refresher, you could dictate a paragraph occasionally to test his recall. Use the same paragraph that you use for spelling, just don't say the punctuation marks or capital letters when you read it. Have him add them. After you have had a chance to look at his work, tell him how many errors you found (like three missing commas or one missing capital letter) and let him find them.

5. Start *Saxon* math lessons.

You have made a great decision to switch to *Saxon*. He said that he struggles with math because the equations are hard, and he doesn't understand them. With Saxon, he *will* begin to understand equations, and since he likes solving mysteries and problems, he might just decide one day that math is his favorite subject!

Count the number of lessons in the text, and add the number of tests. Take this total and divide it by 34 weeks (allow two weeks for sicknesses or interruptions in the schedule). The result will tell you how many lessons or tests a week he needs to complete.

Since he is currently frustrated with math, have him do his math lesson before any other academic studies. After a good breakfast, his mind will be alert, and he has the added incentive of getting the toughest assignment out of the way early.

Designate Fridays as "math games" day. He loves playing games, and there are tons of math board games (*Hive Alive* by *Aristoplay*), math software games (*Math Detective* by *Critical Thinking Press*), and math puzzles (Sudoku). If you want to create your own math games, Peggy Kaye has written *Games for Math*, a good book full of ideas for math games.

6. Download the first set of *Mindbenders* software logic puzzles.

Continue playing *Clue*, *Guess Where*, *Guess Who*, and *Scrambled States of America*, but introduce a new tool for solving problems: *Mindbenders* software by *Critical Thinking Press*. These games will challenge him to use his reasoning skills to discover the correct answer. These games get progressively harder, so start with *Mindbenders A* and then purchase more as you need them. Have him solve two puzzles a week.

7. Have him memorize and recite poetry.

He does fabulous impressions, so take advantage of his listening skills. Go to "LibriVox" on the web and search the site for "poems that every child should know" to access 81 free recordings of a 1904 poetry anthology which contains such famous children's poems as *The Charge of the Light Brigade* and *The Raven*. There are several historical poems from which to choose including selections about Napoleon, Robert Bruce, and Hiawatha. There is an audio player in the upper right corner of the webpage. Show him how to click on the stop button so that he can work on a phrase and the play button for when he is ready to resume listening. Have him listen to an assigned (or chosen) poem until he has it memorized.

He should be able to master three or four poems during the semester depending on the length of the poem. Arrange a family gathering when he is ready, let him share what he has been working on, and clap exuberantly for his effort!

8. Watch the *IEW Student Writing Intensive* DVD series as soon as possible.

This action step is for you! Take time now to watch the four DVDs included in the *Student Writing Intensive*, level C (SWI-C) by the *Institute for Excellence in Writing* (IEW). Do as many of the exercises as you can afford so that you will be equipped to teach him how to write a proper paragraph, how to key word outline, how to add dress-ups, how to add sentence openers, how to add decorations, and how to add triples. Introductions, conclusions, and clincher titles are also covered.

Go to the IEW website and access the free lesson plans. Teach him the concepts gradually by incorporating at least one formal writing session a week. Start small. His hand cramps easily from too tight of a grip, and he already has distaste for writing, so you need to make this fun and easy. Don't ask him to write from any text other than the *IEW* free lessons or the examples in the *Teaching Writing with Structure and Style* teacher manual. Once he masters the process of key word outlining, he will be able to tackle other texts like his science or history texts, but stick to the simple examples that *IEW* provides for now.

If you think he can handle the assignments on the DVDs, let him watch them. He will probably love Andrew Pudewa's humor, and he might decide that writing is cool.

9. Avoid history survey texts; look for history stories.

Decide on a theme or time period that you want to cover with the younger kids. Spend several weeks exploring this theme through library visits. Take the kids every week. Show them how to search the card catalog. Look at all the narratives, biographies, and historical fiction that are available for your particular theme or time period, and choose your favorites to take home that week.

For instance, you might want to learn about the following themes: kings and queens, knights, soldiers, marketplaces, housing, or technology. Start chronologically (oldest first) and read about the theme as it played out in different cultures and at different times. If you want to focus on a particular time period like the Middle Ages, pull all your stories from those years. You should read the history selections out loud to them, and make sure that you ask them to narrate back their understanding by asking the standard "who, what, when, where, how, and why" questions. If they can't sit still while you read, give them something to do with their hands like playing with some clay, a rubber ball, or drawing. Don't assign tests, quizzes, or writing assignments. Make history a pleasant, relaxing experience.

Kenneth's Weekly Plan

- Listen to one book a week and practice reading it out loud with feeling

- Continue reading abridged classics and completing comprehension questions

- Participate in a weekly spelling bee

- Punctuate a dictated paragraph weekly

- Complete math lessons Monday-Thursday and play a math game on Friday

- Solve two mindbenders puzzles a week

- Write one paragraph a week

- Select history books from library for Mom or Dad to read out loud

- Memorize 3-4 poems

Progress Report

Sometime around the end of the semester, take an inventory with Kenneth of his progress. Ask him what he has and has not enjoyed about the plan. If there were steps that did not work for Kenneth, eliminate them from the next semester and come up with an alternative plan.

Pull all of his work and take a big picture look at whether his skills have improved especially in dramatic oral reading, math competency, and basic paragraph construction. Let him assess his own skills and suggest steps for continued improvement. Keep working on those areas that need improvement.

Chapter 39
Exuberant Energy Abounds

A delightful, cheerful little seven year old, Morgan loves playing imaginative stuffed animal games with her brothers. She is an avid reader finding time every day for Ramona, Ralph, Ribsey, and many other fictional friends. She loves being in the kitchen with Mom or big sister, and her favorite recipes involve cookies and cakes. Although she hasn't begun formal piano lessons yet, she is a good singer and might want to learn how to play guitar one day. Weekly skating provides a fun opportunity for putting her exuberant energy to good use!

Mastery Status

Morgan has a rich grasp of vocabulary as demonstrated in conversation and in reading difficult excerpts. She is an excellent reader, so many of the concepts of the English language that still need to be taught will be familiar to her in context. For instance, the eight parts of speech, if taught in the course of daily life using her current books, should be fairly easy to comprehend and apply because she will recognize common sentence structures.

Additionally, organizing thought, solving problems, and recording observations are priorities in this plan as she improves her critical thinking skills. Finally, unstructured play time is still very important, so any learning that can be achieved informally is best. Therefore, skills one and two of the classical trivium (language and thought) will be the focus of Morgan's semester plan.

Morgan's semester priorities:

READING SKILLS

How to read
How to spell
How to write
How to punctuate and capitalize
How to use proper grammar

THINKING SKILLS

How to arrange data according to systems
How to solve problems
How to analyze literature

SPEAKING SKILLS

How to maintain a conversation
How to give a speech

Action Steps

1. Select a chapter book to read out loud to her at least three times a week.

An adept young reader, Morgan pauses at commas, and her pronunciation is precise and accurate. When she runs across vocabulary that she doesn't recognize, she sounds it out in her head to get the proper syllabication and phonetics. Although she prefers not to read out loud because it takes longer, do continue reading to her and including her in adult conversations. Consistently hearing sophisticated language patterns will naturally improve and increase her vocabulary, comprehension, and pronunciation skills.

She is already reading chapter books on her own, so select one classic to read to her at least three times a week. Select a book that is above her grade level. She likes stories about personified animals and children; here are a few favorites that you might try:

Mrs. Frisby and the Rats of NIMH, Robert C. O'Brien
The Trumpet of the Swan, E. B. White
The Cricket in Times Square, George Selden
Where the Red Fern Grows, Wilson Rawls
Caddie Woodlawn, Carol Ryrie Brink

All five of the above suggested books feature both male and female characters, so you could include older brother in this reading time, too.

Before you begin the book, teach her how to preview a book and make predictions about the story line. Look at the pictures on the front cover and read the comments on the back cover. If it is a hardbound book with a book jacket, read the inside flaps together. Look at the book's title, scan the table of contents, and flip through the pages looking for any little illustrations that might provide clues as to the plot. Casually introduce the elements of fiction (character, setting, plot, climax, themes, etc.) throughout the reading whenever you sense a prime opportunity to teach.

2. Hold a spelling bee, or dictate a paragraph.

Her vocabulary is advanced for her age which is probably due to the fact that reading is her favorite subject, and you regularly talk and play with her. Well done! She likes games, so make spelling fun by holding a weekly spelling bee by selecting 10 or 15 words from her abridged classics and have her spell them. Provide a treat for a job well done. Magnetic letters on the refrigerator are another way for fun spelling; just give her a word from the cookbook, and ask her to spell it!

Additionally, you could dictate one quality paragraph a week from her abridged classic. Read slowly while she writes what you are reading. After she is done, circle the spelling errors and have her correct them. If you see a pattern over time (one particular spelling or punctuation rule being broken), take time to teach her the proper rule and let her practice getting it right. For example, four letter words that have a vowel in the 2nd position and an 'e' at the end in the 4th position usually make the vowel have a 'long' sound. Give her some words to spell that follow this rule like "cape, fine, and hope." Don't forget to quiz her on the exceptions, too.

3. Let her supply the missing punctuation.

Type a short paragraph from her reading. Make sure that you increase the font and double space so that she has room to edit. Leave out all punctuation marks. Have her find them. The ones that she misses are the ones that you need to teach. In the beginning, expect her to find all the missing periods, question marks, and exclamation points. Commas and semicolons might stump her, but you love grammar, so you will help her identify the proper usage!

Here is a borrowed idea: create a running story that needs punctuation. Think of an exciting or funny opening sentence like "Heaven forbid! I forgot to…" except leave out the punctuation. Tell her how many punctuation marks are missing and have her find them. Each day, add to the story by writing a new sentence or fragment without punctuation. Repeat the procedure so that she is on a mission to find the missing punctuation and capital letters.

As she masters her punctuation, vary the procedure by writing sentences or fragments that are incorrectly punctuated, and let her find the errors. You could also let her come up with the new sentence or fragment and test your skill for fun. By the way, the goofier the story line, the more fun this game will be.

4. Teach her the grammar concepts in context.

Grammar theory can be very boring to a young child. In fact, she is already learning proper grammar by soaking up the adult conversations and reading quality writing. However, if you want to introduce the basic eight parts of speech, do it in context.

When defining and illustrating, you should group nouns, pronouns, and adjectives together. Teach her that a noun is a person, place, or thing. Have her find the nouns in the room, while driving in the car, or on the campsite playground. Teach her that pronouns take the place of nouns; her stuffed animal is an "it" instead of a "he" or "she." (She might disagree for now if she pretends her pals are real with gender and very busy lives!) Teach her that adjectives modify or describe nouns, so have her add a descriptive word to the nouns she sees around her. For example, on the camping trip she could see a "shiny" pebble, a "decayed" log, or a "hungry" raccoon. She will enjoy coming up with creative adjectives.

Group verbs and adverbs together. Teach her that a verb is an action or being word. Let her demonstrate action: while skating, running, hiking, camping, or cooking. Teach her that adverbs modify verbs, so ask her to show you slow skating or fast skating or reckless skating or careful skating.

Prepositions, conjunctions, and interjections can all be taught as well; just remember real-life illustrations followed by her own illustrations will be more meaningful to her and make learning English grammar more fun.

5. Have her play analogy jeopardy.

Completing analogies will refine Morgan's ability to infer or transfer a property from one subject to another. There are lots of free analogy games online. Pick one game a week for her to play. *Quia* has several online jeopardy games which she will enjoy. When you land on the home page, find the search tool, and enter "analogies" for a list of all the games.

6. Start *Saxon* math lessons.

Math is her least favorite subject because she finds it difficult, so have her do her math lesson before any other academic work. After a good breakfast, her mind will be alert, and she has the added incentive of getting the toughest assignment out of the way early.

Count the number of lessons in the text, and add the number of tests. Take this total and divide it by 34 weeks (allow 2 weeks for sicknesses or interruptions in the schedule). The result will tell you how many lessons or tests a week she needs to complete.

Designate Fridays as "Math Games" day. She loves playing games, and there are tons of math board games (*Hive Alive* by *Aristoplay*), math software games (*Math Detective* by *Critical Thinking Press*), and math puzzles (Sudoku). Older brother will enjoy playing with her. If you want to create your own math games, Peggy Kaye has written *Games for Math*, a good book full of ideas for math games.

7. Take her on a weekly "discovery" trip.

Intentionally plan a weekly field trip in the neighborhood or surrounding area for the purpose of discovering, classifying, describing, comparing, and contrasting. Before you go, create a chart (5 x 6 grid) on a blank piece of paper where she can record her observations. This chart can be copied for all future trips.

For instance, if you are going to the park where you might see lots of dogs, label the horizontal rows "size, sound, color, fur, and breed." Put your own dog, Jake, in the first column as an example. Fill in the data for Jake.

Have her write "dog one," "dog two," through "dog five" at the bottom of each column. Show her how to fill out the categories like you did for Jake. You can do this discovery exercise anywhere. At the local bookstore, have her classify and describe the covers, sizes, textures, photos, and font of red books. At the botanical garden, she can record all that she sees about the lovely flowers. If the weather prohibits a trip, pull out a life science encyclopedia, and have her select mammals to chart.

8. Continue assigning abridged classics for her private reading time.

She enjoys the current reading program and comprehension questions, so continue to encourage daily reading. Since she likes the prewritten comprehension questions, you can continue to assign them, but eventually you want to wean her off of the canned questions and have her ask her own questions. As you read the chapter book to her, you can show her how to ask the standard six comprehension questions: who, what, when, where, why, and how. If you get in the habit of doing this with her, then she will naturally ask the same questions when she is reading alone.

9. Teach her how to write personal letters.

You may already be doing this, but if not, show her how to write a thank you note when she receives a gift. Find a pen pal for her to write; home school students live all over the world, and you may be able to spark an interest in another part of the world in addition to teaching how to write letters. The Yahoo group, *"Home School Form Share,"* has a group of parents who arrange pen pals for their kids; if you join, post a thread asking for a pen pal, and see what happens.

10. Avoid history survey texts; look for history stories.

Decide on a theme or time period that you want to cover with the younger kids. Spend several weeks exploring this theme through library visits. Take the kids every week. Show them how to search the card catalog. Look at all the narratives, biographies, and historical fiction that are available for your particular theme or time period, and choose your favorites to take home that week.

For instance, you might want to learn about the following themes: kings and queens, knights, soldiers, marketplaces, housing, or technology. Start chronologically (oldest first) and read about the theme as it played out in different cultures and at different times. If you want to focus on a particular time period like the Middle Ages, pull all your stories from those years. You should read the history selections out loud to them, and make sure that you ask them to narrate back their understanding by asking the standard "who, what, when, where, how, and why" questions. Don't assign tests, quizzes, or writing assignments. Make history a pleasant, relaxing experience.

11. Have her memorize and recite three stories.

She enjoys drama, so find some short picture books with dialogue to have her memorize and recite to the family. Have her read the book out loud in short sections, repeat the dialogue with feeling, and commit it to memory. Discuss characterization with her so that she represents each person or animal in the story uniquely.

She should be able to master three stories during the semester. You can choose Bible stories, adventure stories, animal stories, or any number of themes. Let her bring home several possibilities from the library and practice out loud until she decides which one she wants to tackle.

Morgan's Weekly Plan

- Listen to one book a week and make predictions

- Continue reading abridged classics and completing comprehension questions

- Participate in a weekly spelling bee or find the spelling errors in a paragraph

- Punctuate a dictated paragraph weekly

- Complete math lessons Monday-Thursday and play a math game on Friday

- Play analogy jeopardy

- Record observations from field trip

- Find a pen pal and write letters

- Select history books from library for Mom or Dad to read out loud

- Memorize three stories or selections with dialogue

Progress Report

Sometime around the end of the semester, take an inventory of Morgan's progress. Ask her what she has and has not enjoyed about the past few weeks. If there were steps that did not work for Morgan, eliminate them from the next semester and come up with an alternative plan. Also remove any steps that seem redundant or that she has mastered.

Pull all of her work and take a big picture look at whether her skills have improved especially in grammar, observation, and problem-solving. Think of small steps for continued improvement that you could do with her over the next semester. Keep working on those areas that need improvement.

Chapter 40
Action Steps for John and Rebecca

In order to ease the classical transition, I prepared a comprehensive "to-do" list for John and Rebecca. In this list, I have taken the action steps for both children and segregated these steps into (a) one-time tasks like purchase books and (b) recurring tasks like weekly reading.

Once John and Rebecca have had a chance to digest both strategic plans, they can decide what suggestions they will implement and allocate the work amongst themselves. There are certain teaching goals that John is best equipped to handle while other teaching goals are clearly in Rebecca's domain.

Preliminary ONE-TIME Action Steps

- ❑ Watch the *IEW* writing DVDs
- ❑ Create an observation chart for Morgan's field trips
- ❑ Purchase *Mindbenders* software, set A, for Kenneth
- ❑ Show Kenneth how to use the audio player on *LibriVox*
- ❑ Teach Morgan how to write personal letters and find a pen pal for her

RECURRING Action Steps

With your 11 year old:

- Read to Kenneth with feeling or give him an audio book (once a week)
- Teach Kenneth a different writing concept (once a week)

With your 7 year old:

- Read a chapter book to Morgan and show her how to predict (3 times a week)
- Create a running story that needs punctuation for Morgan (daily)

- Teach Morgan the eight parts of speech and the elements of fiction
- Show Morgan how to play analogy jeopardy (once a week)
- Help Morgan find three stories or selections to memorize for recitation

With both your 11 and 7 year olds:

- Take Kenneth and Morgan to the library and on a field trip (once a week)
- Hold a spelling bee or dictate a quality paragraph for Kenneth and Morgan (weekly)
- Teach Kenneth and Morgan their math (4 times a week)
- Play math game with Kenneth and Morgan (once a week)
- Read history narratives, biographies, or historical fiction to Kenneth and Morgan (weekly)

Second Family

&

Joe, Anne, Three Sons,
and Two Daughters

Chapter 41
Practical Jokes and Secret Chuckles

While not exactly high school sweethearts, Joe and Anne graduated from the same alma mater and had mutual friends. The similarities stop there, though, because their individual experiences in private Christian high school were like night and day. Bored with all the busy work, Joe expressed his frustration by clowning around while Anne breezed through with straight A's...although she secretly chuckled at Joe's shenanigans.

While pursuing two undergraduate degrees, one in business and one in industrial engineering, Joe served six years as a radio communications specialist in the U. S. Marine Corps. Anne took a position as a registered nurse in a metropolitan city 600 miles from home. Eventually, Joe tracked her down, and they finally became true sweethearts. Married for fourteen years, Joe and Anne are the parents of five children: Tom (12), Lauren (10), William (8), Christy (5), and Brian (6 months).

Although Joe was aggravated with the conveyor-belt mentality of traditional education, he did not let his first experiences get in the way of real lifelong learning. Wanting to go back to school, he recently found an excellent Executive MBA program which allowed him the flexibility to be a full-time Dad and breadwinner during the week while studying and attending classes over the weekends. Armed with a graduate degree and shunning the restrictions of employment, he and a partner donned entrepreneur caps and started their own internet server business which generously provides for all of the family's financial needs.

Pediatric nursing was perfect training for Anne because she loves children and has a gentle, quiet demeanor. Her peaceful spirit is translated daily in the home through kind words of encouragement and tender touches whenever one of her children passes by. She never complains and rarely raises her voice in anger, but her children know when she means business. Family is extremely important to Anne. She is very close to her siblings, parents, and in-laws and manages frequent gatherings to foster close friendships between cousins, aunts, uncles, and grandparents. She enjoys singing, reading, cooking, and making her home a pleasant, quiet retreat for family and friends.

Anne has read some books on classical education and finds the idea intriguing, but she wonders how in the world you can do a classical education with five young children. Spend a few minutes getting to know her better by reading her responses to my questions about home education before you meet her children and read their strategic semester plans.

When were you first introduced to the idea of home schooling?

> I first learned about home schooling as a high school student when I babysat for a family that taught their children at home. I started to have friends that adopted home schooling about 11 years ago.

Why did you decide to teach your kids at home?

> We wanted our children to have a great education, we wanted them to love learning, but most importantly, we wanted them to be with us so that we could teach them to love the Lord with all their hearts, souls and minds.

How long have you been home schooling?

> We've been home schooling for six years.

What moments related to home schooling have brought you the greatest joy?

> Just having the TIME with my children has brought such joy! We have had many, many conversations that may not have taken place without the time that we spend together. I have been able to be there when the Holy Spirit was working in the lives of my children and we have been able to pray right then and there.

What moments related to home schooling have brought you the most frustration?

> I have been frustrated trying to juggle all of my responsibilities as mom, wife, and teacher. I have also been frustrated teaching math!

How organized would you say your home school is?

> Our home school is moderately organized.

How structured is your typical day?

We follow a routine, but not an hour by hour schedule.

Do you take breaks throughout the calendar year?

We do take breaks, and we somewhat follow the public school calendar, but we do not in any way feel bound to it. My father had open heart surgery a few years ago followed by a stroke. We took several weeks off at that time so that I could help with his recovery.

Do you have a dedicated room just for school?

Yes, but it is because we have the space available. It is great to have a room to organize your stuff, but we really do school all over the house.

What general areas do you feel qualified to teach?

I have just finished getting one child through elementary school, so I would say I feel qualified to teach that.

Are there any areas of study in which you feel inadequate?

As we plunge into the Jr. High years, I am feeling a little more inadequate. It is more a question of balancing the education of four kids - this is where the inadequacy comes in!

Are there other things that you want to teach them that you haven't had time to do yet?

Yes! I would like to go deeper with Latin, writing, geography, history...we have done some of all, but it is never enough!

What is your biggest concern or question about giving your kids a classical education?

Trying to accomplish this with five children!

* * * * *

Now let's meet four of Joe and Anne's five children: 12 year old son, Tom; 10 year old daughter, Lauren; 8 year old son, William; and 5 year old daughter, Christy.

151

Chapter 42
Artistic Precision Prevails

Tom exhibits two unusual qualities for a twelve year old boy: extreme accuracy in observation which is then precisely translated into artistic representation. He and a few friends are collectively producing a movie that uses miniatures, and he has created the set from scratch. Precisely carved stone walls slope just like a real stone wall; the distribution of matter takes gravity into account so that the wall sits perfectly still without wobbling. The tiny action figures come from the wholesaler colored in gray, so Tom meticulously applies colorful paint (without a magnifying glass!) so that the edges are exact. Engineering and architecture immediately come to mind when marveling at his creative work.

Excelling in all areas of learning with little apparent effort, he, like his father, has a tendency to become bored and wonders why he needs to perform certain tasks. This semester his parents have enrolled him for the first time in a structured classroom setting of other home school kids who meet twice a week to learn together. Tom will be taking math, science, literature, and one elective, Adobe PhotoShop.

Mastery Status

Tom has substantially mastered the English language, the first skill set of the classical trivium. Thought, skill number two, will be improved in his ongoing math and science studies as well as the completion of the logic puzzles. Up until now, he hasn't spent much time learning how to communicate orally (other than conversations) or in writing, skill set number three. His biggest priority for the coming semester should be learning how to consistently produce a concise, one-idea paragraph. Although he is enrolled in an upcoming literature class, he has read one of the primary texts already, so the semester plan includes one major classic in addition to the outside class assignments. This classic is purely optional; he is mentally and linguistically ready for the challenge, but if it interferes with his other work, postpone the reading until a future date.

Tom's semester priorities:

READING SKILLS

How to read
How to write
How to use proper grammar

THINKING SKILLS

How to arrange data according to systems
How to solve problems
How to analyze literature

SPEAKING SKILLS

How to write a paragraph
How to give a speech

Action Steps

1. Give him responsibility for little brother.

Select one day a week, and have Tom thoughtfully select an appropriate book to read aloud to little brother. Supervise his selection, and suggest that he pick a topic that interests both brothers. Make sure that he selects a book with grammar and vocabulary that is above little brother's own reading level.

If he selects literature, encourage him to look for a boy's adventure chapter book like *Robin Hood*, *Treasure Island*, or *Peter Pan* which they can read together over several weeks. Literature should be read aloud with feeling so that little brother hears variations in pitch, pacing, and volume that convey the author's intent. Tell him to pretend he is an actor, and consider how much more he enjoys a vibrant performance than a dry, flat one.

If he is more interested in reading nonfiction, have him select a theme that meets your objectives for both boys. For instance, since Tom is so gifted in the area of physical science, he could select a unit on pulleys, levers, and inclined planes. Tom could create a unit study that not only involved reading the text and looking at the diagrams but actually building a model of the machine.

2. Assign a classic piece of literature, and coordinate with history reading.

Since he is such an advanced reader, and literature is his favorite subject, he is probably ready to delve into the supervised study of the classics. History is his second favorite area of study, so pick a classic that can be integrated with history. Homer's *Iliad*, translated by Richard Lattimore, is a heroic tale of battle and adventure. Weapons, military strategies, and slaughters abound, so he should enjoy it! Themes like honor, strength, nobility, and selfishness percolate through the story and provide lots of material for discussion. The *Odyssey*, also by Homer, is lighter and has more humor and less battle. These texts were both originally narrated aloud by a professional storyteller, so it might help his comprehension to read the text out loud although it will take longer to do it this way.

Optimally, Dad would read the classic, too, on his own time so that they could discuss each book (there are twenty-four books or "chapters") together. Dad might see themes and ideas that he wants to explore on a deeper level. In the event that Dad cannot participate, find a neighbor or friend who would be willing to read it with him. At his age, expect a full semester spent on this one piece of literature.

Since the *Iliad* is an epic of Ancient Greece, Greek history would be a logical area for further reading. He is not ready for a complete survey of Greek history, but he could select certain events or cultural facets to explore like the Persian Wars or the Peloponnesian Wars. Greek weapons would also be a natural fit. Make sure that you keep track of his work in Greek History and Literature so that you can record it on the high school transcript for credit. Drop the *Story of the World* reading and the *Story of the World Activity Book* from his requirements.

3. Have him memorize one speech from the Bible for recitation.

Stephen's speech in the *Acts of the Apostles* (chapter seven) summarizes the history of Israel and the Gospel in fifty-three verses. Have him read the entire piece out loud first then write all fifty-three verses out in longhand. If he were to work on a verse a day, he could memorize the entire speech by the end of the semester. There are several different methods for memorizing, but we have found that repetition works the best. We call our method "see it, say it, hear it, write it."

4. Discontinue his formal grammar lessons.

His grammar education is nearly complete; this is probably attributable to the fact that he reads good literature and that he completed years of grammar drill. The only areas of grammar that he cannot easily define are advanced concepts related to the properties of verbs:

- verbals (participles, gerunds, and infinitives)
- conjugation (progressive, emphatic)
- voice (active v. passive)
- mood (indicative, imperative, subjunctive)

He will pick up these concepts through good reading choices and naturally incorporate them in his writing later on. Unless he is planning on a career as a writer or an editor, he doesn't need to know the technicalities of verb properties.

5. Discontinue Latin until he decides to pursue it for high school credit.

Although he could begin a high school Latin course of study at this age, he will be dealing with some integration and study skill issues as he pursues the new math text (*Saxon*) and science text (*Apologia*) in the formal classroom, so put Latin on hold until he is adequately acclimated to the new environment and requirements.

6. Purchase the downloadable *Mindbenders* software.

Critical Thinking Press produces a series of logic puzzles called *Mindbenders* which get increasingly more difficult as the student advances. You can download them directly to your computer's desktop so that they are easily accessible. Have him complete one or two puzzles a week if he has time.

7. Require a polished written paragraph three times a week.

He already knows how to key word outline, write from the outline, and add all six stylistic dress-ups (strong verb, -ly word, quality adjective, who/which, www.asia, because). Make sure that he turns in a key word outline for his history and literature reading. Proofread and edit his rough draft. Have him add six dress-ups, if possible, to every paragraph. After he creates a clincher title, have him print a final copy and grade himself. Purchase a typing program so that he can easily make corrections to his draft, and discontinue the cursive writing workbook.

Writing a concise, one-topic paragraph is his weakest area, so you need to make this a priority. He needs to quickly come up to speed if he is interested in debating next year because so much time is devoted to learning debate theory and research skills that he won't have time to learn how to write the constructive debate argument, and he would get very frustrated. Even if he doesn't participate in debate, he needs to master the stylish single paragraph so that he can move on during the next semester to multiple paragraph essays with transitions, introductions, and conclusions.

8. Teach him self-discipline by giving him a weekly schedule.

Sit down with him at the beginning of the academic year and go over your expectations with him in detail: memorize a speech, read a classic, etc. Help him allocate the work over the semester so that he generally knows what needs to be done on a weekly basis. For example, he is going to write three paragraphs a week for you. He is going to memorize fifty-three verses of Scripture, so over twelve weeks, he would need to memorize four or five verses a week.

Tell him that you are going to try something new in that you are going to let him choose how and when to complete his work for the week. Choose a loss of privilege beforehand so that if he fails to deliver, he is not surprised by the consequences. Give him a deadline for turning in the work (Friday night, Sunday afternoon, or you could ask for certain parts throughout the week as completed). If after a few weeks you find that he is not ready for the responsibility, don't punish him; just go back to giving him daily assignments until you think he is ready for more freedom.

Tom's Weekly Plan

- Read to William (once a week)
- Read one classic (daily)
- Read history (once or twice a week)
- Memorize Stephen's speech (daily)
- Solve one *Mindbender* puzzle (once a week)

- Write concise, one-idea paragraphs from history (three times a week)

- Complete *Saxon* and *Apologia* assignments (daily)

Progress Report

Sometime around the end of the semester, take an inventory with Tom of his progress. Ask him what he has and has not enjoyed about the past few weeks. If there were steps that did not work for Tom, eliminate them from the next semester and come up with an alternative plan.

Pull all of his work and take a big picture look at whether his skills have improved especially in basic paragraph construction. Let him assess his own skills and suggest steps for continued improvement. Keep working on those areas that need improvement.

Chapter 43
Little Mother-in-Training

Lauren is a little mother-in-training, but she's only ten years old! When her newest baby brother joined the family six months ago, she eagerly stepped right up to help Mom with all the obligatory duties like changing diapers and catching dribbly burps. Lauren can often be seen planting a gentle kiss on baby's cheek, but Lauren does not lavish her attention exclusively on the newest member of the family. She also quietly shepherds her younger brother and sister who are eight and five years old, respectively, with a serene assumed authority that shows respect instead of the typical older sibling dominance.

In addition to mothering skills, Lauren is learning how to cook. She has mastered the recipes for snicker doodles and sugar cookies. She doesn't need Mom's help in the kitchen for these goodies; she just pulls out all the necessary ingredients and begins to work. Lauren's grandmother supervised her first sewing project, and she wants to learn how to create other garments soon.   —

Mastery Status

Lauren has an excellent command of vocabulary which is not surprising because she loves to read. Most of the work planned for her in the area of skill set number one, language, is designed to review what she already knows in the areas of capitalization, punctuation, and grammar. The bulk of her time can now be spent in sharpening her thinking (skill number two) through natural observation and description, solving problems and logic puzzles, and discussing the elements of fiction. She is familiar with the basic paragraph and some stylistic methods, so she can begin working on skill set number three, speech.

Lauren's semester priorities:

READING SKILLS

How to read
How to spell
How to write
How to punctuate and capitalize
How to use proper grammar

THINKING SKILLS

How to arrange data according to systems
How to solve problems
How to analyze literature

SPEAKING SKILLS

How to write a paragraph
How to give a speech

Action Steps

1. Give her responsibility for little brother.

Assign one day a week as her day to read aloud to little brother. Her organization skills are strong, so she might enjoy creating a reading plan for the semester that focuses on one children's author like Michael Bond (*Paddington Bear* series), Beverly Cleary (*Henry Huggins* series), or Mary Pope Osborne (*Magic Tree house* series). Or she might want to concentrate on reading a different classic fairy tale or fable to little brother each week. Hans Christian Andersen wrote 159 tales, and there are over 600 fables passed down from the storyteller, Aesop, which should provide her with plenty of stories from which to choose. If she decides to go with Aesop, she'll need to read more than one in a sitting since his fables are shorter than the Andersen fairy tales.

Literature should be read aloud with feeling so that little brother hears variations in pitch, pacing, and volume that convey the author's intent. Tell her to pretend she is an actress, and consider how much more she enjoys a vibrant performance than a dry, flat one. Reading with feeling not only helps little brother internalize good reading habits so that he can imitate them, but it also develops her future public speaking skills.

2. Assign a fiction series for reading, discussion, and journaling.

Since she reads the *Little House on the Prairie* series by Laura Ingalls Wilder and *The American Girl Doll* series, she must enjoy following favorite characters through various plots. She is an excellent reader for her age, so she is ready to move on to a series with harder vocabulary and more complex sentence structure. The following selections are arranged from easy to difficult.

Books by George Selden:

The Cricket in Times Square
Chester Cricket's New Home
Chester Cricket's Pigeon Ride
Harry Kitten and Tucker Mouse
The Old Meadow

Books by George MacDonald:

The Princess and the Goblin
The Princess and Curdie

Books by Kathryn Lasky, Kristiana Gregory, and others:

Dear America Series—biographical diaries
Oregon Trail
Voyage on the Great Titanic
Great Depression
Gold Rush

Of course, if she hasn't read C. S. Lewis' *The Chronicles of Narnia* or Brian Jacques' *Redwall* series by herself, now is the time to let her read them on her own. She can probably handle one series or four to six books over the course of the semester.

Have her read every day, preferably early in the day and right before bedtime. Purchase a lovely little "reading journal" for her to record her thoughts. Every time that she reads a chapter, she should jot down a few thoughts; if she can summarize the chapter in a sentence or two that would be good training for later. Teach her to ask the standard questions (who, what, when, where, how, and why) as she's reading.

3. Teach her the elements of fiction.

Walk her through the elements of fiction (character, setting, plot, climax, theme, conflict). You might want to select one element a week to teach in detail. Explain the element then have her write about that particular element for two to three weeks in her reading journal. For instance, explain plot (the problem exposed, rising action, climax or turning point, falling action, and conclusion), then have her take notes in her reading journal for two weeks on plot. Make time each week to have her bring her reading journal to the table, pour a cup of tea or milk, and have her share her discoveries with you.

4. Reduce her English grammar and spelling workload.

Her spelling and grammar skills are very good; she is nearly equal with her older brother in understanding all but the most advanced grammar concepts. If you want to continue using the grammar and spelling workbook, keep an eye on her performance so that you can eliminate unnecessary drill and move on to the next concept. In other words, if she is consistently demonstrating mastery over a unit concept, call it "complete," and assign the next unit. Less busy work will free up time for more reading and composition.

5. Dictate one passage a week to her.

Take the current fiction book that she is reading, choose a paragraph, and slowly read it out loud so that she can copy it down. Do not include any punctuation clues other than natural pausing or inflection. Let her capitalize and punctuate. Have her go back over her work and edit. Teach her to use a red marker and proofreading symbols to find capitalization, punctuation, and spelling errors. This may sound backwards from the traditional workbook method of teaching capitalization and punctuation, but it will serve to show both you and her rules she needs to master. Before having her copy the corrected paragraph read her corrected copy and add anything that she missed.

You can also use this method to assess her knowledge of English grammar. Instead of having her add the capitalization and punctuation, have her identify the eight parts of speech (noun, verb, adjective, adverb, preposition, conjunction, pronoun, interjection). Don't require identification of all eight in one sitting. Focus on finding all nouns, pronouns, and adjectives one day, all verbs and adverbs another day and all prepositions the next week.

6. Eliminate the cursive handwriting workbook.

Her cursive is beautiful. Drill out of context is just busywork. If you want her to practice her cursive, have her choose a paragraph from her current reading to copy in her best cursive, or require her to use her cursive in all of her formal writing assignments so that she gets "real-life" practice. Since the reading journal thoughts are more free-flowing, she can print these notes which will probably be quicker for her.

7. Have her memorize four short poems or song lyrics for recitation.

Find a collection of children's poetry, and let her choose four poems to memorize. If she prefers songs over poetry, find an old hymnal (great theology) most of which have four verses each. In this case, she would memorize four hymns.

Have her read the entire piece out loud first then write all the verses out in longhand. Work on one verse at a time, and keep layering on new verses, saying the old verses, too. So on day one, she will only memorize and recite verse one. On day two, she will memorize verse two, and say both verses one and two. On day three, she will memorize verse three and say all three verses. She can start with the first verse and work her way to the end of the poem or hymn, or start with the last verse and work her way to the beginning of the poem or hymn. When she has mastered the poem, gather the family around and let the recitation begin.

8. Discontinue Latin until she decides to pursue it for high school credit.

Although you may have heard that Latin is essential to a real classical education, elementary Latin texts are taught out of context and only teach unrelated vocabulary. She would unlikely learn enough Latin vocabulary to significantly improve her understanding of unfamiliar English vocabulary. Translations at this age are short and pointless. Wait until she is ready to learn the entire Latin grammar so that she can translate real texts like Cicero and Caesar.

9. Purchase the downloadable *Mindbenders* software.

Critical Thinking Press produces a series of logic puzzles called *Mindbenders* which get increasingly more difficult as the student advances. Have her complete two puzzles a week. She can do the same puzzles as her older brother although he might move through them more quickly.

10. Continue regular math lessons.

You have made a good decision to adopt *Saxon* math. Take the number of lessons in the book plus the number of tests; divide this total by four. This will tell you approximately how many weeks it will take to complete the book. You might be able to get by on three lessons a week, but since she loves math, she may want to do it every day. If so, assign her four *Saxon* lessons a week (say Monday through Thursday) then designate Fridays as "real-life" math days.

On real-life math days, teach her how to do things like measure the bathroom for wallpaper or paint, figure the total cost of gasoline pumped or miles per gallon, and subtract entries in your checkbook. Since she enjoys cooking so much, let her create the shopping list, gather the items at the grocery store, and estimate the total bill. Teach her to comparison shop by looking at the labels on the shelves with unit prices. Have her learn measurements by cooking. Even though she loves math, Fridays will seem like a treat because she gets to apply what she is learning in fun activities.

11. Practice observation and prediction skills on regular field trips.

Since her little brother will be going on regular field trips to develop his critical thinking skills, use these opportunities to teach her to hone her own observation and prediction skills. Purchase a sketchbook, a canvas tote bag (she can decorate it with stencils and paint), and some colored pencils just for her. Have her take her supplies every time that you go on a walk or field trip. Show her how to find something interesting in nature to record in her sketchbook.

Sketch a detailed drawing (say a flower, tree bark, a parked airplane, or an historical costume) and color it later. Write a brief description of any particularly interesting details. If the item lends itself to change, have her predict what will happen next. For example, perhaps she has found a butterfly on the bush in your front yard. Have her run through some possibilities for his next action.

Formal science instruction is not really useful until she has mastered the three skills of the trivium and is ready for the supervised study of subjects. If she wants to read about science, let her pick random topics to explore in short doses.

12. Require a polished written paragraph once a week.

Teach her the concept of a good paragraph (one idea expressed in a single topic sentence and three-five supporting sentences) by having her draft and polish one concise paragraph a week. She is already familiar with the concept of a key word outline and the six dress-ups (strong verb, -ly word, quality adjective, who/which, www.asia, and because), so now it is time to put her exposure into practice.

Select one chapter from *Story of the World* or any other library book on history. Make sure you select a narrative instead of a fact-filled encyclopedia. You want an original source paragraph that demonstrates one idea; many of the children's illustrated encyclopedias combine random ideas in what looks like paragraphs, but are not "one idea" paragraphs. Either random events or a particular period from history will work for this exercise because the point is primarily to learn how to write - not how to catalogue history.

Have her read the passage, and key word outline three to five points (three words per point). Then have her close the book and draft her paragraph from the key word outline. Make sure that she double spaces so that she has room to add her dress-ups or make spelling corrections. Once her draft is complete, have her add six dress-ups if possible. If not, make sure she adds a quality adjective, a strong verb, and an –ly word at a minimum. Have her rework the last sentence so that she can repeat the clincher title. Finally, have her rewrite the entire paragraph for publication on the refrigerator.

Lauren's Weekly Plan

- Read to William (once a week)
- Read one fiction series or 4-6 books (daily)
- Keep notes in reading journal (every time you read)

- Complete grammar and spelling exercises (weekly)
- Edit dictation paragraph (once a week)
- Memorize four poems or hymns (daily)
- Solve *Mindbender* puzzles (twice a week)
- Complete four *Saxon* assignments (max) a week
- Do real-life math (once a week)
- Sketch in nature journal (once a week)
- Write one history paragraph (once a week)

Progress Report

Sometime around the end of the semester, take an inventory with Lauren of her progress. Ask her what she has and has not enjoyed about the past few weeks. If there were steps that did not work for Lauren, eliminate them from the next semester and come up with an alternative plan.

Pull all of her work and take a big picture look at whether her skills have improved especially in dramatic reading, descriptive observations, problem solving, and basic paragraph construction. If you feel that she has reached mastery in language, drop the dictation and devote more time to solving logic puzzles. Keep working on those areas that need improvement.

Chapter 44
He Never Meets a Stranger

Relationships are crucial to eight year old William. He loves to talk, and nothing pleases him more than receiving the undivided attention of family and friends. He frequently calls his cousins on the telephone and stops by his friend's home for a quick chat or a video game. In a busy family of seven, there is not often time for social gatherings, but William reminds his Mom when they need to invite friends to dinner or for a play date. Because he thrives on meaningful conversation, William has developed excellent listening and verbal skills. He is very bright and has lots of pertinent knowledge to share.

Not only does William have aural and verbal skills, but he also has amazing visual ability. He doesn't like to draw from the imagination, but when he draws from a picture, his imitation is as good as or better than the original. He enjoys soccer, piano, and video games.

Mastery Status

William's oral communication skills are advanced for his age. Usually, a child masters skill set number one (language) and number two (thought) before moving on to effective speech, but William has leapfrogged the standard pattern to begin perfecting his public speaking skills. When he is finally ready and able to write effectively, he will be a dynamite debater, lawyer, or professor. Although his articulation and vocabulary are good, he does need to work on speaking with feeling, so the majority of his work over the next semester relates to listening to quality reading and practicing reading out loud.

William's semester priorities:

READING SKILLS

How to read
How to spell
How to write
How to punctuate and capitalize
How to use proper grammar

THINKING SKILLS

How to arrange data according to systems
How to solve problems

SPEAKING SKILLS

How to maintain a conversation
How to write a paragraph
How to give a speech

Action Steps

1. Read to him once a day.

Have someone read, with inflection, to him daily. Mom and Dad don't have to be the only ones who read to him. Big brother and sister can each take a day a week to read as part of their required reading. Pick a topic that is interesting to him in any area of knowledge, or have brother or sister read from their assignments. Don't confine yourself to literature, but do look for narratives that have dialogue or can be read with feeling. Consider giving him a smattering of topics, or focus on one particular area of interest. If you cannot squeeze in live reading, give him a cassette or mp3 audio file to listen to.

Give him something to do with his hands while he is listening like a rubber ball, a squeeze toy, some building blocks, modeling clay, or colored pencils and a sketchpad. Teach him to preview a book by looking at the front cover, back cover, pictures, and title. Ask him to make a prediction about the story based on your preview evidence, and congratulate him at the end when he is correct.

2. Give him responsibility for little sister.

Commit to a weekly library trip so that he can pick five to ten books for two purposes: (1) nighttime pleasure reading and (2) reading to his younger sister. I sense that he puts pressure on himself to act older like his brother, so he may balk at selecting picture books (too babyish), but tell him that you are giving him a big responsibility now that he is getting older for teaching little sis how to read. Encourage him to select simple, colorful narratives for his little sister's sake. If he wants to read short chapter books for his own pleasure at night, let him, but don't push him beyond the picture books for now.

Put a light by his bed, and send him upstairs 30 minutes before "lights out" (Sunday through Thursday) to wind down and "preview" the picture book that he will read to little sis the next day. Tell him to read it once to himself and think of ways he could make it exciting (sound effects, dramatic pauses, volume changes—you might have to show him). Tell him to think of at least two questions to ask her about the book before, during, or after reading. For instance, he could flip through the pictures with her and ask her to predict what's going to happen in the story, or he could ask her to tell him her favorite character. Teach him how to use his finger to point to the words while he's reading to her.

The next morning, have him read the book out loud so that he can practice reading it with feeling. It might help him avoid possible embarrassment if he goes to a quiet place like the backyard, the front stoop, the library, or the bathroom (the mirror is a good place to practice facial expressions) where he can relax and practice alone. Finally, have him sit down with little sister and read the book with feeling. Tell him to talk to her about the story and not to forget his two questions. Tell him that just like big brother and big sister report back to you after reading to him, you expect him to tell you how their reading time went, too.

3. Have him explain one story a week to you.

Select one of the stories, whether read to him or by him, to narrate once a week. After the story is over, have him tell you what the story was about. You can ask him questions to get him started if he is reluctant or doesn't know where to start. Take down his thoughts as if you were taking dictation. Then select one or all of the sentences that he gave you (depending on your judgment of how much copying he can take), and copy his thoughts on double-spaced, wide-ruled notebook paper. Make sure that you copy in longhand, not cursive.

Create a narration page for him. A sketchpad, copy paper, or notebook paper will do as long as you divide the page from top to bottom as follows: the top 2/3 is left blank for his illustration and the bottom 1/3 is lined for his writing. If you choose to use notebook paper, make sure that you give him wide ruled paper. If you use a sketchpad, you'll have to draw the lines each time. You could make a template on a blank page then make 36 copies at Kinko's. Have them bind it or hole punch it and put them in a folder so that you have a record of his progress throughout the year.

Give him your copy of his narration along with the prepared narration page. First, tell him to copy (longhand) his words on the lines, being careful to do his best work and stay between the lines. As he is copying, you can point out the punctuation to him and explain its usage. Next time he sees that punctuation mark, you can ask him what it is used for. You can also use this opportunity to teach simple sentence structure like declarative, interrogative, imperative, and exclamatory sentences.

Next, tell him to use the upper 2/3 of the paper to illustrate the story any way he wants. At first, let him draw anything or copy from the book. Later on, you can encourage him to think about drawing the main ideas or characters. Let him color the drawing if he wants. Finally, ask him to think of a catchy title for his narration. Write down his title, underline it, and then have him copy it at the top of the page over the illustration.

Every budding author needs an audience, so make it a habit to share his work with siblings, Dad, and grandparents. If he thinks that other people will be reading and commenting, or if he thinks he will have to read it to someone, he will do his best work.

4. Have him practice his sight words.

Determine his knowledge of sight word list A. There are 100 words on each list (appendix), and they progress from easy to difficult. First, ask him to read list A out loud. Then decide how you want to teach the sight words that he doesn't know. You could create a concentration game with note cards, or you could create a free, easy crossword puzzle. (Search for "Eclipse Crossword" on the internet.) If you drill verbally, make sure that you give him something to do with his hands while you quiz him. I would probably only work on 10 or 15 words at first until he masters them. Make sure that you point them out in the books that you are reading to him whenever you see one. When he masters list A, move on to list B. When he masters list B, start on list C.

5. Teach him the English spelling rules.

His pronunciation is good, so I don't think you need to spend much more time on phonetics. Since he will be narrating once a week and copying your dictation, this is a good time to focus on the spelling rules. When you see a word in his narration that you can use to teach a rule like how to form a plural or a superlative, point it out to him. Let's say that you found a comparative in his narration and want to teach the spelling rule that you take the adjective and add the suffix "-er" to compare the two adjectives. You teach this rule in several ways. Take a blank piece of paper and write the noun from his paper at the top of the page. Now add a plus sign, the suffix –er, an equal sign, and the comparative adjective like this:

quick + er = quicker

Then have him think of other comparatives to write on the list like this:

quicker
faster
slower
tighter

You can also create games for teaching spelling rules. Bingo cards are easy to make, and you can use beans or coins as counters. Several websites allow the free creation of custom cards. Put several words that follow the rule on the card and every now and then have him tell you the rule when he lands on a word. You can also make crossword puzzles, or use a *Scrabble* game or magnetic refrigerator letters to have him duplicate the words that follow the rules. Once he's gotten the rules down, you can move on to the exceptions if you think he's ready.

In addition to teaching spelling rules, he might enjoy a regular spelling bee as his vocabulary increases. Select 10 words from his reading and announce the word to be spelled. Find something small for him to hold while he stands before you. Tell him that he is to repeat the word both before and after he spells it. Arrange for a little goodie for performing well.

6. Select three pieces for him to memorize and recite.

Over the next semester, select three multiple line pieces for him to memorize. He is extremely verbal, so he should enjoy this activity. Instead of having him memorize individual verses of Scripture, have him memorize the narrative stories of the Bible. This will take a little work from Mom or Dad initially. Find a favorite story from the Bible like David and Goliath, Jonah and the big fish, or Noah and the ark. Read the Scripture passage; write your own abstract of the passage adding dialogue if you want to make it more exciting. He will memorize your text.

Read the text to him initially then have him read the entire piece. Every day have him read one new line out loud with inflection; he will add a new sentence each day to the old sentences that he already knows. If he wants to memorize greater portions of the text, by all means, encourage him to go as fast as he wants. When he is ready to recite the piece, collect an audience of siblings and neighbors, and let him entertain them with his rhetorical skills!

Bible stories are not the only things he can memorize. Aesop's fables, civic myths like Ben Franklin's discovery of electricity, or poetry are also good choices for his age. Humor and dialogue are not necessary, but they would help him practice adding emotion for the audience's sake. Eight year olds generally like to tell jokes or riddles, so maybe you could find a few books at the library and help him pull together enough to give a three to five minute recitation.

7. Capitalize on his keen observation skills.

He is extremely observant, so take advantage of his ability to copy pictures and listen in on conversations by going on a weekly field trip. As he practices classifying, describing, and comparing, he'll improve his thinking skills. Take a small sketchbook and a pencil, a camera, or a voice recorder. Have him record what he sees. You can show him how to create a three column chart to record his observations with tally marks if you want.

Decide on a topic and pick a skill. For instance, if you walk around the neighborhood, you might want to classify houses. Find a characteristic that is quantifiable like brick, stone, or wooden siding, and have him keep a running count of the quantities. Also have him sketch or photograph the three types. If you go to the local commuter airport, he can practice describing the types of propeller airplanes in terms of material, number of passenger seats, or number of seconds that it takes them to take off. Have him record his findings. You could go to the car dealership and have him compare (find similarities) and contrast (find differences) in the cars for sale on the lot. Again, have him record, draw, or photograph his findings.

Another exercise for building thinking skills that he might enjoy is outlining how things work. Teach him how to verbally outline, step by step, how the things around the house work. Then have him write down the steps using the numbers 1, 2, and 3. Start with easy appliances like the toaster and move on to more complicated machines like the lawnmower.

8. Continue moving forward with his math lessons.

Regular math lessons and problem sets will establish good problem-solving habits and solidify the concepts in his mind. He is doing well with his addition and subtraction skills, so work on his multiplication and division skills until he has mastered all the times tables. I would not do more than four lessons a week and use Fridays for math games. There are lots of books available (*Games for Math*, Peggy Kaye) if you want to create your own math games, or you can use computer games that you purchase (*Critical Thinking Press*) or find for free online. If your math text calls for manipulative aids, make sure you purchase these.

William's Weekly Plan

- Choose 5-10 books to read to Christy (once a week)
- Think of two questions to ask Christy from that day's reading (daily)
- Read the book out loud once alone (daily)
- Read the book out loud to Christy (daily)
- Narrate and illustrate one story (once a week)
- Read final narration to family at end of week
- Complete sight words puzzle (even week)
- Play spelling rules game (odd week)
- Participate in spelling bee (once a week)

- Memorize three Bible stories (daily)

- Take a weekly field trip and record observations

- Write down the steps for how something works (occasionally)

Progress Report

Sometime around the end of the semester, take an inventory with William of his progress. Ask him what he has and has not enjoyed about the past few weeks. If there were steps that did not work for William, eliminate them from the next semester and come up with an alternative plan.

Pull all of his work and take a big picture look at whether his skills have improved especially in reading out loud with feeling and narrating story content. If he is reading with more drama, scale back a bit, but if he is enjoying reading to his sister, by all means, encourage this practice. Keep working on those areas that need improvement.

Chapter 45
A Faithful Friend

Five year old Christy loves to be outside whether playing soccer, climbing in her tree house, or affectionately petting every puppy that comes along. When inside, she is either playing with her Webkins and American Girl dolls or drawing pictures from her imagination. She endears herself easily as evidenced when she recently moved into a new neighborhood where she quickly made friends of all ages. One striking feature of Christy's personality is her willingness to sacrifice what she wants for the good of the group or for specific friends. When other little girls demand that their game be played, she cheerfully agrees without grumbling or complaining. She shows her affection with a simple touch and enjoys a big hug.

Mastery Status

Christy almost knows the entire lowercase alphabet, with the exception of a few typical confusing letters like b, d, and p. She can sing the ABC song and writes her first name legibly. She is very good at classifying and matching games. Counting to ten is no problem for her. Skill number one, acquiring the language, is the primary thrust of her semester plan. She is eager to "read" and will greatly benefit from all the reading that her parents and siblings shower on her.

Christy's semester priorities:

READING SKILLS

How to read
How to spell
How to write

THINKING SKILLS

How to arrange data according to systems
How to solve problems

SPEAKING SKILLS

How to maintain a conversation

Action Steps

1. Read to her three times a day.

Morning, noon, and night are all good times for reading books! Decide on what reading session big brother will take, then Mom and Dad can take the other two times to read colorful picture books to her while snuggling on the sofa, in bed, at the kitchen table, or on a blanket in the yard.

Show her with your finger how the text moves from left to right. Occasionally point out simple words and repeat the letters like this:

> "See this word? This is the word for 'dog." Dog is spelled 'd-o-g.' Can you spell dog? Use your fingers to point out each letter as you say it."

Start by pointing out short, three letter words of the same phonetic pattern (like cat, hat, bat, rat), then move on to the first 100 sight words. Use lots of inflection. Pause at commas. Raise your voice for questions and exclamations.

Monitor William's progress with Christy on a frequent basis. Make sure that he is reading with inflection, that he has practiced reading the book the night before, and that he is asking her at least two questions about the book.

2. Teach her the lowercase alphabet.

She already knows most of the ABC song. Like most kids, she gets a little messed up at 'l-m-n-o-p.' Teach her the names of the letters along with the sound. Describe the shapes as you write the letter for her. For instance, if you are teaching the letter 'b,' you could say:

> "To make the letter 'b,' you draw a straight line down from top to bottom then add a round belly from the halfway point to the bottom of the line."

Let her practice making her letters after you show her how. Purchase a sketchbook or have Kinko's bind 30 blank pages with a spiral trim. As you work on a letter, have her add the letter to her ABC book. Add the lowercase letters to the left page of a two page spread, and leave the right page blank. When she has learned her lowercase, you'll come back and add the uppercase letter on the right side.

After she writes her letter on the blank page, give her a magazine, some child-proof scissors, a glue stick, and have her cut out photos of things that begin with the letter to paste on the letter page. Keep doing this until she fills the book with all 26 lowercase letters then teach her the uppercase letters and do the same thing with the ABC book.

3. Teach her how to build words.

Explain to her how a collection of words are put together in sentences and end with a period. Tell her that this may seem like new information, but she already knows this because she has been talking in sentences ever since she was little girl. Tell her that you and William are going to teach her the secret code for solving the reading puzzle.

When she knows most of her letters and a growing list of sight words, the time to start building words has arrived. Work with one root at a time. Look for the "Phonetic Roots" table in the appendix.

For instance the two letters '-a' and '-t' when put together make the sound 'at.' All you have to do is add a consonant at the beginning to make different words. Get a blank piece of paper. Write the letter combination 'at' in a vertical column down the paper several times. Then write all the consonants that you can think of that would make a word with 'at' across the top of the page. Give her a pencil, and have her build her own words by adding a new consonant to each line of 'at.' Let her pronounce each new word. Have her show Dad when he gets home how she is learning to break the code by reading her new words.

If you want to teach her a few three letter verbs using the phonetic roots (like 'ran' or 'hop'), you can show her how to write a simple sentence like 'Christy ran.'

4. Give her a picture book to "read" each night before bed.

When you go to the library, let her pick out as many picture books as she wants for her bedtime "reading." Put a cute little basket just for her books by the bed. Send her upstairs 30 minutes before lights out, and tell her this is a special treat just for big kids.

Tell her to use her new code-busting skills to discover letters and words that she recognizes. Don't require any work; this reading time should be pure pleasure.

5. Keep introducing higher and higher numbers.

She is counting from one to ten with no problem. Gradually introduce each new set of ten working your way up to fifty. Show her that all numbers, no matter how big, are only put together with the numbers 0-9. Write the numbers 1 through 10 on a piece of paper, and keep adding tens (11-20; 21-30; etc.) under the prior set of ten like this:

1	2	3	4	5	6	7	8	9	10
11	12	13	14	15	16	17	18	19	20

Count whenever and where ever you are: in the kitchen, in the car, or on a walk. Give her some dry beans, and have her make piles of ten. Tell her to put her crayons into piles of ten. Have her create two mounds of pebbles of different quantities. Encourage her to count mailboxes on a walk or flowers in a bed.

Continue progressing through the *Explode the Code* books. She is learning how to classify, observe similarities and differences, and recognize patterns. She seems to enjoy matching the similar pictures and circling the ones that don't belong, so keep using these texts as long as she remains engaged with them. Once she gets bored, move on. If you are certain that she understands the concept, you don't have to complete the book. A formal math text is not necessary yet.

6. Reserve lots of time for play!

Don't worry about her reading, writing, and computing skills yet. She is only five years old, and she will learn so much through simple play. Although she wants to "do school" like her older brothers and sister, don't let her spend too much time at the table doing seat work. Tell her that home school kids learn all day long and all over the house and yard!

7. Continue teaching her good manners and proper conversational skills.

She is an adorable little girl well on her way to proper etiquette and conversation. Teach her how to talk on the telephone to cousins, grandparents, and strangers. Occasionally listen in on her conversations with her dolls, her siblings, and her neighborhood friends so that you can nip any potential problems in the bud. Teach her how to write a thank you note by letting her dictate her words of gratitude to you while you copy them down then let her sign her name.

Christy's Weekly Plan

- Learn lowercase alphabet
- Make an ABC book
- Count to 50
- Play inside and outside
- Dictate thank you notes and sign

Progress Report

Sometime around the end of the semester, take an inventory of Christy's progress. Has she learned all of her lowercase alphabet? Is she starting to recognize certain simple words in the text? How high can she count? Keep reading and working on those areas that need improvement.

Chapter 46
Action Steps for Joe and Anne

Four strategic plans could be overwhelming, so I prepared a comprehensive "to-do" list for Joe and Anne. In this list, I have taken the action steps for all four children and segregated these steps into (a) one-time tasks like purchase books and (b) recurring tasks like weekly reading.

Once Joe and Anne have had a chance to digest the four strategic plans, they can decide what suggestions they will implement and allocate the work amongst themselves. There are certain teaching goals that Joe is best equipped to handle while other teaching goals are clearly within Anne's expertise.

Preliminary ONE-TIME Action Steps

❑ Purchase sketchbooks and colored pencils for Lauren and William
❑ Purchase the *Iliad* or the *Odyssey* for Tom
❑ Purchase the *Mindbenders* software from *Critical Thinking Press*
❑ Purchase a book basket for Christy's library books
❑ Bind 30 pages of blank copy paper for Christy's ABC book

❑ Teach Lauren how to write a concise, one-idea paragraph
❑ Teach William to preview and predict a book
❑ Teach William how to outline steps of a process

❑ Create a narration page for William
❑ Test William's knowledge of the 100 sight words
❑ Select and summarize three Bible stories for William to memorize
❑ Gather magazines for Christy's alphabet book

* * * * *

RECURRING Action Steps

With your 12 year old:
• Help Tom establish his weekly goals

179

- Discuss the classic literature reading with Tom (weekly)

With your 10 year old:

- Teach one element of fiction to Lauren (once a week)
- Dictate one paragraph to Lauren (once a week)

With your 8 year old:

- Read to William daily (Anne twice, Joe once)
- Monitor William's reading to Christy (daily)
- Copy down two sentences from William's narration (weekly)
- Create a sight word puzzle for William to complete (bi-weekly)
- Create a spelling game for William to complete (bi-weekly)
- Hold a spelling bee for William (weekly)
- Play a math game with William on Fridays

With your 5 year old:

- Read to Christy twice a day (Anne or Joe)
- Teach Christy her lowercase alphabet (daily)
- Help Christy create her alphabet book (daily)
- Teach Christy how to build words (after she masters ABCs)
- Work with Christy on recognizing her numbers and counting (daily)

With your 10, 8, and 5 year olds:

- Take the kids to the library (once a week)
- Take the kids on a field trip with sketchbooks (weekly)

Third Family

&

David, Ruth, and Eleven Children

Chapter 47
Almost an Even Dozen

A large house is just what this family needs! David, father of four adult children, met and married Ruth when she only had two sons: Jack and Todd. Since then, this blended family has fruitfully borne two more sons (ages 4 and 2) and three daughters (ages 9, 6, and 4 months). Recently their family has grown even larger as Ruth's mother has moved in with them after experiencing some health issues, so David, a "jack of all trades," is building a new home for his expansive family. The oldest boys are helping David with construction.

When he is not working on their new home, David spends his time as an electronics technician. Generally he works from 8 a.m. to 5 p.m. unless his employment takes him out of town. Once he had a four hour round-trip commute! Additionally, in his line of work there is always the possibility that he may have to leave during the week and return on weekends which would not be too burdensome on Ruth since she does most of the teaching while David guides her decisions and sharpens her understanding.

Although David thinks he is not a good teacher, he has ably immersed Jack (age 13) in his love for electronics; Jack has gladly embraced David's passion and might apprentice with his step dad when he gets a little bit older. Not surprisingly, post-World War I history documentaries are a favorite pastime because of the fascinating advances in technology. David enjoys audio books in the genres of science fiction, biographies, and history.

Ruth certainly has her hands full as the caretaker of seven children, a husband, and her recovering mother, but she cheerfully accepts her calling with a peaceful countenance. She may not get a lot of private downtime, but when she can sneak a few minutes for herself, she loves creating digital scrapbook pages. Ruth loves the fact that there is no mess to clean up! Ruth's mom, her mentor, taught her how to quilt; she has completed handmade quilts for each of her kids with one exception, and that quilt is still a work-in-progress.

A lifelong learner, Ruth always thought she would become a teacher, but after she received her Associate's Degree in Elementary Education, she decided that she didn't want to teach in the public school system. Now she has her own students to teach! She is thinking about going back for her Bachelor's Degree one day, and if she does, she will probably pursue an English major with a minor in Language.

Ruth describes her approach to home schooling as relaxed. Being an A student all her life, she wants her kids to reach certain levels of academic achievement, but she also knows that young children learn so much simply by playing. Spend a few minutes getting to know her better by reading her responses to my questions about home schooling before you meet her children and read their strategic semester plans.

When were you first introduced to the idea of home schooling?

My aunt and uncle taught their children at home, and a couple at church did, too.

Why did you decide to teach your kids at home?

I wanted our family life to revolve around God and our family, not the public school's schedules. I did not want my children exposed daily to the things that I remember being exposed to in school. I wanted my children to be able to learn at their own pace, in their own way, and with a focus on what they desired to learn about (within reason). After much prayer and discussion with my husband, we decided it would be the best course for our family.

How long have you been home schooling?

We have been home schooling for eight years.

What moments related to home schooling have brought you the greatest joy?

Last week my eleven year old son read an entire section of a book about bats with much less difficulty than usual. My children often come to me to have me help them with a discovery they have made or are trying to make. I love it when they "get" something important, such as a biblical concept and can relate it to their lives.

What moments related to home schooling have brought you the most frustration?

I am most frustrated when I have to figure our new ways to explain a concept because they just aren't "getting" it, when they aren't learning on my timetable, and when they don't do assigned work and tell me it is because it isn't "fun." When I don't set a good example for them and get the day started, we end up not doing anything for the day...all of these situations frustrate me.

How organized would you say your home school is?

On a scale of 0 to 10, our home school organization is about a 4.

How structured is your typical day?

On a scale of 0 to 10, our typical day is structured about a 4.

Do you take breaks throughout the calendar year?

We try to school year round taking unscheduled sanity breaks and breaks during major holidays.

Do you have a dedicated room just for school?

We are building a new house which has a room just for school, but where we are right now at the old house, no.

What general areas do you feel qualified to teach?

I feel qualified to teach history, math (through Algebra 2), science (except physics), Bible, and reading instruction.

Are there any areas of study in which you feel inadequate?

Foreign language (including Latin and Greek), writing, literature (in particular analysis), and grammar are areas in which I feel inadequate.

Are there other things that you want to teach them that you haven't had time to do yet?

I want to teach them writing, grammar, foreign language, literature, and memorization. We tried "Classical Writing," and everyone including me hated it. We tried *Latin's Not So Tough* (LNST), *Latin Primer*, and *Latin Grammar* (both *Canon Press*). LNST was too

185

worksheet driven and *Canon Press* was just over my head to teach. In literature, I want to teach literary analysis.

What is your biggest concern or question about giving your kids a classical education?

Will we ever get to the point where they love learning and are able to educate themselves in all areas necessary to fulfill their goals and mission?

* * * * *

Now let's meet four of David and Ruth's eleven children: 13 year old son, Jack; 11 year old son, Todd; 9 year old daughter, Alice; and 6 year old daughter, Teresa.

Chapter 48
Robots and Circuit Boards

With an eager, intelligent mind, 13 year old Jack passionately consumes knowledge about chemistry, physics, and electronics. When he reads for pleasure, he usually reads nonfiction about his three passions. When he has free time for puttering around the house, he creates projects like a tone generator and a memory counter with his Radio Shack electronic learning lab. He builds circuit boards with his step dad and uses computer software to write code. Building robots is also fun for him.

Jack has already designed several inventions which he keeps in a special folder. First, he "builds" the idea in his head, and then he draws it on paper and files it away for future use. When he earns spending money, he purchases the necessary parts to build prototypes of his inventions. At this time, he is thinking about a career in engineering, and he might officially apprentice with his step dad when he gets a little older.

Jack enjoys science fiction and the technological aspects of history. Strategy games like *Age of Empires* and *Runescape* engage his imagination; he is even systematic in his approach to these games in that he writes out his plan for his quests.

Mastery Status

Jack has substantially mastered his English language skills (classical trivium skill number one) with the exception of some advanced grammatical concepts. The bulk of his time during this semester will be spent improving his thinking (skill two) and speaking (number three) skills primarily through reading, writing, discussing, and performing scientific experiments.

Jack's semester priorities:

READING SKILLS

How to write
How to use proper grammar

THINKING SKILLS

How to solve problems
How to structure and analyze arguments
How to use the scientific method
How to listen

SPEAKING SKILLS

How to write a paragraph
How to give a speech

Action Steps

1. Gradually reintroduce formal writing on a weekly basis.

Sometimes it is good to take a break from tasks when both you and he are getting frustrated, so your sabbatical from formal writing was a good decision. However, Jack needs a few years to develop solid writing skills if he is going to pursue the higher level science careers, so it is time to reintroduce the structured paragraph.

Some writing curricula try to do too much in the beginning like teaching the child how to interpret meaning while teaching basic structure. He needs to focus on structure first using content that is interesting to him. The prior content was distant and detached from his daily life, so asking him to write with meaning about content that he found meaningless was a futile pursuit that would drive an adult crazy, too.

His interests are almost exclusively related to chemistry, physics, and electronics, so use his passions as a springboard for his writing topics.

Creative writing is probably not something that he would enjoy unless it was a science fiction piece, so teach him the standard nonfiction paragraph and three point essay. Given his interests in the field of science and technology, he will probably end up doing technical writing one day if he writes at all. A career as a novelist is less likely than a chemical engineer.

Teach him how to outline a science topic using key words then draft a single topic paragraph. Once the draft is complete, show him how to vary the sentence structure and add stylistic dress ups. Have him print the final copy and grade himself using a simple checklist:

- Is the paragraph about one idea?
- Do all the other sentences support that one idea?
- Did I add all six dress-ups?

To illustrate, assume he is reading an encyclopedia article on lasers. Let him select one topic to outline; he could choose the history of lasers, how lasers work, or what lasers look like. Some encyclopedias will give you clues about the topics by using subheadings. Show him how to read only that one section of the text and outline the main points.

Key word outlining is an easier method than Roman numeral outlining. Have him read one sentence and pick three words from the sentence (usually nouns and verbs) that will remind him what the sentence was about. Write the three words on the paper. Move on to the next sentence and pick three words. Write them down. Do this for all the sentences in the text that relate to his one idea. Close the encyclopedia and have him narrate (to you) his one-idea paragraph from the key word outline.

Now that you know he understands the topic, tell him to draft the one-idea paragraph from the key word outline. Make sure he has a topic sentence and that all other sentences support the idea of the topic. Follow this procedure for four or five weeks until he is comfortable key word outlining and drafting a one-idea paragraph from a nonfiction text.

Once he has mastered this step (the structure of a one-idea paragraph with a topic sentence and supporting ideas), show him how to vary the sentence structure and add stylistic techniques using his prior draft paragraphs. Take the first paragraph that he wrote and tell him to add the following dress-ups:

1. an '–ly' word (adverb)

2. a quality adjective
3. a strong verb
4. the word 'because'
5. 'www.asia' word (when, while, where, as, since, if, or although)
6. 'who' or 'which'

He may not be able to add all six dress-ups, but he should be able to add at the least the first three. After he has added the stylistic dress-ups, have him type the entire paragraph (double spaced) and print a final copy. Let him grade himself. Do this for every remaining week of the twelve week period until he has mastered key word outlining a single idea paragraph from a nonfiction text.

If he demonstrates that a stylish one-idea paragraph is easily achievable, ask him to prepare three paragraphs on a related topic and tack them together with an intro and conclusion. (These ideas are taken from the *Institute for Excellence in Writing* materials if you want to learn more.)

2. Purchase a typing text for him.

Boys generally prefer typing their essays because editing punctuation, spelling, and grammatical errors is so much easier in *Microsoft Word* than rewriting the entire essay in longhand. Although he has had some informal experience with typing on the computer by participating in the *Runescape* chats, he needs a simple program that teaches him the entire keyboard in a few weeks. *Type It*, by Joan Duffy will take what he already knows about the keyboard and fill in the blanks. The lessons are short and reinforce phonetic and spelling rules. Have him do a few pages twice a week.

3. Have him dictate one paragraph a week to his younger sister.

He is not really interested in reading fiction literature, so do not assign any classic lit at this time. Additionally he had a bad experience with ancient classic literature when completing his prior writing program. However, there is a way to expose him to quality literature while organically teaching the advanced grammar concepts which he still needs to master. Again, he hated the formal grammar course that you used before, so how can you teach him advanced grammar without a textbook? Unless he is going to be an English teacher or professional writer, he really doesn't need to know the proper terms such as gerunds, participles, and dangling modifiers; he only needs to know how to use them properly in his writing.

Quality fiction is one of the best ways to learn English grammar, so have him dictate a paragraph from his younger sister's assigned reading on a weekly basis. He will read it slowly to her, including punctuation marks, so that she can copy down what he says. Have him check her spelling, too.

The classics are not limited to literature or philosophy; there are classic writings in the sciences that you can introduce when he gets a little older. He may enjoy reading the original source documents for Galileo's astronomical discoveries and Euclid's geometrical theorems among other classics.

4. Continue with his current math coursework.

He is enjoying the current math text and problems, so don't make any changes here. Have him grade his own work and correct any errors.

5. Capitalize on his budding inventive mind, and teach him how to write claims.

He is already keeping a file for his potential inventions, and he's researched U. S. patent law, so it could be that he will eventually obtain legal patents for himself. Let him go to the United States Patent and Trademark Office webpage (uspto.gov), search the database for terms in which he is interested (say 'electronic devices'), and click on a few links to see what a real patent looks like in terms of structure (abstract, history of the invention, claims, illustrations, etc.) Claims are simply step by step descriptions of the components of the invention. He could write mock patents for each of his inventions as preliminary steps to obtaining the authentic legal rights to protect his inventions.

6. Teach him how to record his observations using the scientific method.

He is enjoying his general science text, but other than his electronics projects, he has not yet performed any laboratory experiments. Janice Van Cleave has published easy science lab books for all branches of science from engineering to astronomy, so go to your local library or find used copies of her books and do a weekly experiment in the kitchen. Her experiments can be done with normal household supplies.

Give him a notebook for his labs and show him how to fill in the following steps:

1. Observe and identify the problem
2. Form a hypothesis (prediction)
3. Design and perform experiment
4. Collect and analyze data
5. Conclude whether hypothesis stands or falls

Retest if the experiment fails.

7. Consider entering him in a robotics competition.

The *National Robotics Challenge*, held annually in Ohio, and *RoboFest*, held annually in Michigan, are just two of many possible robotics competitions. If you search on the internet, there are hundreds of robot competitions around the USA which you could investigate. Even if you decided not to participate in a formal tournament, you could learn how to host your own local tournament with other home school students by reading these websites.

Find a few other home school friends who are interested in building robots, and get together regularly to tinker and learn. You don't need expensive parts, but if you want to go in together on a kit, *Gears Educational Systems* and *LEGOeducation* both carry supplies.

8. Assign a few scientific discoveries for memorization and recitation.

Have him select a few scientific discoveries, summarize the story in narrative form, write it out, and memorize it. Have him memorize a line or two a day, continuing to layer on new lines, by reading his narrative out loud in front of the bathroom mirror with feeling. Tell him to pretend that he is telling the story to little children or that he is acting on a stage. When he is ready to perform his recitation, gather the family and cheer his efforts.

9. Have him watch history documentaries with his step dad.

You can find full length historical documentaries at the local library, on television, or even on the internet. Decide on a theme or time period that is interesting to both your son and husband. Perhaps they want to learn about weapons and the progression of technology. Find 10 or 12 videos that include this theme, and let them watch one a week. Or maybe they agree that World War II is fascinating, so look for movies on this time period. Even regular movies can be informative when integrated with historical documentaries. Encourage them to discuss the content of the documentary after it's over. There is no need for formal history texts at his age unless he prefers reading that type of nonfiction.

10. Introduce a beginner's inductive Bible study for his quiet time.

He is probably ready for meatier Bible study now, and since you are familiar with the Kay Arthur *Precepts* series, purchase one of her beginner's inductive Bible studies, *Discover 4 Yourself Children Series,* for him to use in his morning quiet time. There are lots of choices (Joseph, Daniel, Abraham, how to pray, God's names), and they may seem too easy for him, but they will teach the basic concepts of inductive Bible study without overwhelming him.

After he has completed a few of the easy studies, he may be ready to join a local *Precepts* class of other youth or purchase a study to do with you. Inductive Bible study fits right in with a classical Christian education because he will learn how to observe what the Bible says, interpret the meaning in context, and apply what he has learned to his life.

Jack's Weekly Plan

- Key word outline and draft one science or technology paragraph (once a week)

- Complete the typing text (weekly)

- Dictate one paragraph from Alice's literature reading (once a week)

- Continue *Teaching Textbooks* work (weekly)

- Learn how to write patent claims (occasionally)

- Perform laboratory experiment and document using scientific method (once a week)

- Form a robotics group or team

- Select and summarize a few scientific discoveries for memorization and recitation

- Watch history documentaries with your step dad (weekly or biweekly)

- Complete inductive Bible studies (daily)

Progress Report

Sometime around the end of the semester, take an inventory with Jack of his progress. Ask him what he has and has not enjoyed about the past few weeks. If there were steps that did not work for Jack, eliminate them from the next semester and come up with an alternative plan.

Pull all of his work and take a big picture look at whether his skills have improved especially in writing a stylish, concise paragraph and recording his laboratory observations. Keep working on those areas that need improvement.

Chapter 49
Swords of a Blacksmith Wait

Todd is fascinated by medieval history: battles, knights, armor, crowns, castles, and clothing all capture his imagination. This 11 year old has been known to create swords out of cardboard and belt a sweatshirt to make a pages' tunic. A real bow, arrow, and target round out his collection of weapons, but he hopes to learn blacksmithing one day so that he can make his own swords. Sometimes he pretends to be a knight riding his horse while other times he draws cartoon knights.

He prefers books about knights, too, although he does enjoy listening to books on tape about other historical periods like the American Civil War as long as the content has to do with war and soldiers. In addition to creating his own fun, he enjoys playing the computer strategy game, *Age of Empires*; he just completed the Joan of Arc campaign.

When Todd was six years old, he was diagnosed with sensory integration dysfunction along with some eye motor control issues. At that time, he received two years of occupational and physical therapy at the local public school. Until recently, he didn't really have the fine motor skills or prolonged attention to learn how to read or write; however, now he is progressing and is reading at a late first grade/early second grade level.

Mastery Status

To speak with Todd, you would never know that he has struggled with reading and writing. He is intelligent and articulate. His general knowledge base appears comparable to other eleven year olds, so his delayed literacy hasn't gotten in the way of learning. In fact, he is *very* literate about life, but he lacks the concrete reading and writing skills that most eleven olds have mastered. Now that his body is ready to catch up with his mind and spirit, he should focus on the first skill, language, while continuing to improve his thinking (road two) and speaking (road three) skills.

Todd's semester priorities:

READING SKILLS

How to read
How to spell
How to write
How to use proper grammar

THINKING SKILLS

How to arrange data according to systems
How to solve problems
How to use the scientific method
How to analyze literature
How to listen

SPEAKING SKILLS

How to give a speech

Action Steps

1. Utilize voice recognition and transcription software.

Delayed ability to read and write should not hinder his acquisition of language, critical thinking skills, and communication skills. He can still learn how to write a paragraph, identify the elements of fiction, and record his observations and conclusions using the scientific method. However, until he comes up to speed in reading and writing, you'll have to be creative in the form that his record takes. Here are two ideas for creative recording of his thoughts:

a. Purchase a voice recorder

Office supply stores sell inexpensive handheld voice recorders with hard drives; these little devices can be connected to a USB port of the computer. Once connected, your preferred music player (RealPlayer, Windows Media Player, i-Tunes) opens and plays his recorded thoughts. You or one of the other kids can then type his thoughts and print them out. This method is more laborious for family members.

b. Use the built-in voice recorder and typing program in your computer

If you are using Microsoft software, your computer has a speech recognition and transcription capability. Click on "start>control panel>sound speech and audio devices," and you can then use the wizard to customize the "voice recognizer" to his own voice. If you don't already have a headset and microphone, you'll need to purchase one. He will speak into the microphone, the wizard will initially record data about his voice, and then every time he puts on the headphones to record his thoughts, he can watch the computer record his thoughts in text before his eyes. He'll probably love this.

You can also increase the size of the text for him by clicking on "start>control panel>accessibility." This method increases his self-reliance since you won't have to type his thoughts; you may have to go back in and edit the text though because sometimes the computer cannot distinguish the spoken word correctly.

Of course, these ideas are not permanent solutions, but they should really boost his self-esteem as he will now be able to communicate his thoughts on paper just like his older brother and younger sister. His mind is moving as quickly as any other eleven year old boy, so don't let his visual and sensory difficulties prevent his natural progress. Continue to teach him how to read and write, and when visual literacy finally clicks, he'll be able to record his thoughts with his own hand.

2. Read to him every day.

Have him sit with you and little sister as you read her illustrated narratives. Point out words and patterns as you move through the text. If it is not too much trouble for you to read separate books for him, indulge in books about knights, castles, and medieval adventures. Once a week, have him narrate the story back to you, copy down his words (no more than two to three simple sentences – you can abridge), and have him copy them on a piece of copy paper in his best handwriting.

197

Divide the page into 2/3 blank for his illustration (since he likes to draw) and draw wide-ruled lines on the bottom third so that he can write his own summary from your dictation.

Books on tape won't improve his reading skills, but they will increase his literacy with the spoken word, increase his vocabulary, and teach him proper sentence structure. While you will use lower than grade level picture books to teach reading, you should find grade level or higher books on tape for his private "reading" at night before bedtime.

3. Practice phonics and spelling by using the sight words.

You can use several of the sight words (appendix) to teach phonics and spelling rules. For instance, the word "sat" teaches the short vowel sound for "-a," and the word "hope" teaches that the vowel "-o" is long when the word ends in an "-e." Take these words and have him build new words like bat, cat, and hat or rope and cope. Take a blank page, and write the example word in longhand at the top of the page. Then explain the spelling rule to him. Ask him to go in order of his ABCs and see how many new words he can make with the root. Have him write each new word directly under the prior word so that he can visually see the first consonant changing while the root stays the same like this:

b a t

c a t

f at

Once he learns a few rules, create two or three bingo cards with a mix of the words that he has learned. When he places a bingo bean on a word, have him tell you the rule.

4. Create a word wall.

Decide which words you want to him to recognize. Choose from one of the three sight word lists or group phonetic sounds together. If you have a chalkboard or whiteboard, write the chosen words on the board in a horizontal and vertical grid like the game board used in Jeopardy or Concentration. If you don't have a surface on which to write, purchase blank note cards, and write the words on them. Spread them out on the kitchen table in a grid.

Purchase a new (clean) fly swatter. If he is competitive and responds well to timed games, then purchase an egg timer or use the microwave timer to make the game a race. Have him stand near the word wall when you are ready to begin the game.

Tell him that the objective is to swat the word as quickly as he spots it. Read the word then watch him swat it. If you've ever been to a carnival or amusement park, this game will remind you of the one where the little gopher pops his head up at random, and you have to bonk it with an overstuffed mallet.

You can play this game every week with new words that get progressively more difficult. This game should improve his fluency and word recognition while making reading fun.

5. Play the bell game with him.

Here is another way to improve literacy while improving pronunciation. Decide which words you are going to work on this week, and create index cards with the words clearly written on them. If you are using a phonetic plan for reading to him, use the same words that are in this week's books. Find a portable bell in the house, or purchase one at the dollar store. Those little bells that you tap at the store counter to get the attendant's attention are available at office supply stores, and they are fun to smack, too.

Stack the word cards on the table along with the bell. Explain that in this game, you are going to turn the card over and show him the word. He has to read the word silently then ring the bell when he is ready to pronounce the word. If he pronounces the word correctly, he gets a point. If he rings the bell but then cannot say the word, he loses a point. Decide how long or how many points before the game is won. You could have incentives for high points like level one wins a longer play break, level two wins extra video time on the computer, and level three wins an extra ice cream at dessert. You can also add a time element here if he likes competing against the clock.

6. Purchase grammar songs for him to learn.

Audio Memory sells a great cassette or CD kit that teaches seven of the eight parts of speech (except conjunctions), punctuation, as well as Greek and Latin roots through song. Sixteen songs cover verbs, nouns, sentences, pronouns, compound personal pronouns, adjectives, adverbs, apostrophes, prepositions, direct objects, capitalization, plurals, irregular verbs, commas, quotation marks and Greek & Latin prefixes and suffixes. The great thing about this method is that he doesn't have to be an advanced reader to learn his English grammar. By the time he can identify the parts of speech in a text, he will already be an expert on the purpose for each part.

7. Have him dictate his scientific method findings.

Teach him how to use the scientific method just like you would the rest of the kids, but have him record his hypotheses, observations, and conclusions about the natural world using the computer's voice recognizer and transcription software. If you are doing a laboratory experiment in the kitchen, he can run over to the computer and record his thoughts in real-time. If you are out in the woods, you may have to take notes for him or use a handheld voice recorder. Let him draw any illustrations in longhand and attach them to the printed copy of his thoughts.

8. Teach him the elements of fiction.

Discuss character, setting, plot, theme, and conflict with him using the same ideas that are included in his nine year old sister's plan.

9. Teach him how to "write" a simple one-idea paragraph.

Even though he will not be physically writing paragraphs with his own hands, he can learn the concepts of a topic sentence and a tightly written single idea paragraph as well as stylistic dress-ups. Decide what topic that you want him to "write" about (knights, castles, and weapons would be a good idea from either history or his literature), and have him record his topic sentence and paragraph on the voice recognizer. He might want to print out the paragraph then have you add the stylistic dress-ups manually.

10. Resume his math course work.

Now that you have had a nice sabbatical from regular math, you might want to consider switching to a different math curriculum. *Saxon* math texts are excellent. Since you are not exactly sure how far behind he is for his age, search online for their 18 page PDF placement tests and have him take the primary grades exam. This will take some time on your part, so budget accordingly. You will follow the script and assign points for whether he understands the math concept or not. They provide templates and worksheets for all of the questions, so all you have to do is print out the assessment and assemble the manipulative aids.

Depending upon his total score, *Saxon* will recommend the exact text you should purchase. If you want to introduce math games on Fridays, that might be fun for your eleven, nine, and six year olds.

11. Record a story about knights for him to memorize and recite.

Reading a story about King Arthur out loud would be too labor intensive for him, so record the story on cassette tape so that he can memorize it by listening to your voice. Step dad or big brother could do this for you if you prefer. Have him listen to the recording and repeat the words until he is ready to recite the story with dramatic flair. Gather the family for an entertaining history lesson!

Todd's Weekly Plan

- Read with Mom and Alice (daily)
- Listen to book on tape at bedtime (daily)
- Narrate story to Mom, copy sentences, and illustrate (once a week)
- Select print books and books on tape from library (once a week)
- Build words with Mom (weekly)
- Play "Swat" and "Bell" with Mom (weekly)
- Listen to and learn a new grammar song (every week)
- Record your labs using scientific method on computer
- Complete math lessons with Mom (weekly)
- Write one paragraph a week using voice recognizer (weekly)
- Listen to the story about King Arthur and memorize (until ready to recite)

Progress Report

Sometime around the end of the semester, take an inventory with Todd of his progress. Ask him what he has and has not enjoyed about the past few weeks. If there were steps that did not work for Todd, eliminate them from the next semester and come up with an alternative plan. Pull all of his work and take a big picture look at whether his skills have improved especially in reading and writing. Keep working on those areas that need improvement.

Chapter 50
Joy Animates Her Words

Curiosity is a personality trait that nine year old Alice enjoys putting to use. She is an attentive observer of nature and especially enjoys the anatomy, temperament, and adventures of horses. She loves taking field trips and wishes that she had more time for such fun. The animal kingdom is among her favorite topics, and she is thoroughly enjoying her current reading of Dr. Doolittle and his conversations with the animals.

An excellent reader, Alice articulates her consonants and pauses appropriately at commas. Her voice is very pleasant and sweet with a hint of joyfulness animating the words. She is smart and performs most tasks very well which could be due to the fact that she is not satisfied with mediocrity but pushes herself toward perfection. Alice has an empathetic, servant's heart which is so helpful in such a large family.

Mastery Status

Alice is very articulate for her age, and her vocabulary is strong. She enjoys reading and writing, so much of her semester plan centers on mastering the English language. Additionally, she will be working on skill number two, thought, through her examination of fiction, through her math lessons, and through her observations of nature. Finally, her writing and recitations will establish a good starting point for effective speech (skill number three).

Alice's semester priorities:

READING SKILLS

How to read
How to spell
How to write
How to punctuate and capitalize
How to use proper grammar

THINKING SKILLS

How to arrange data according to systems
How to solve problems
How to analyze literature

SPEAKING SKILLS

How to write a paragraph
How to give a speech

Action Steps

1. Let her select three illustrated books a week to read to little sister.

An excellent reader, she articulates her consonants precisely, pauses at commas, and pronounces unfamiliar vocabulary by sounding out the syllables. Take advantage of her growing skill by having her read three picture books a week to little sister. Take her to the local public library and let her select the books. Since they both enjoy horses, she might want to start with the beautifully illustrated *A Field Full of Horses* by Peter Hansard.

Reading out loud has several tangible benefits. She will be a better public speaker if she starts practicing now. She will enjoy "teaching" little sister how to read. Little sister will enjoy the attention of big sister, and their relationship will be strengthened by this ritual. Little sister will learn good language simply by soaking up the rhythms, pauses, and vocabulary that big sister shares. Finally, you will have more time to spend on other responsibilities.

2. Have her copy a paragraph from dictation weekly.

Every week have older brother dictate a quality paragraph from her literature. A quality paragraph would have various sentence types (simple, complex, compound, or compound-complex), various punctuation (commas, question, apostrophes, or quotation marks), and challenging vocabulary. Have her copy the passage, word for word, along with the punctuation marks on every other line of her paper (double-spaced) so that big brother has room to edit her work.

Next, her older brother should compare her copy to the original and circle any spelling errors, missed punctuation, or capital letters she forgot. Teach him how to use red proofreader's marks like the circle for spelling errors and the strikethrough for lowercase. Search online for good examples. Since she dislikes spelling, this is a good opportunity for big brother to teach her any spelling rules that she consistently misses. He will enjoy the responsibility, and she will benefit from his knowledge. Have her correct her work.

3. Use her weekly dictation paragraph for grammar instruction.

Take the weekly paragraph from her classic literature, and have her substitute the existing nouns, verbs, adjectives, adverbs, pronouns, prepositions, conjunctions, and interjections for her own quality words.

Let's say in week one, you want to reinforce the idea that a noun is a person, place, or thing. After she copies the original paragraph and corrects her errors, have her highlight or underline all the nouns. Next have her think of substitute nouns to replace the existing nouns. She can create a totally different story or find synonyms to keep the story similar. You could teach synonyms and antonyms this way, too.

The following week, teach the concept of adjectives and have her substitute all the adjectives. She can either add the new words on the blank line above the original line with a red proofreading bubble, or you can have her rewrite the entire paragraph with the new words. In subsequent weeks, teach all eight parts of speech. This method of imitating great writing is very effective since the structure is already built so all she has to do is supply the details.

4. Teach her the elements of fiction from the books that she is reading.

Require an hour of quality reading every day. She can read for 30 minutes in the morning then 30 minutes before bedtime, or you can designate a quiet hour in the day for all of the older kids to read or listen to books on tape. Make time in your schedule to debrief on a weekly basis. Ask her to tell you about the most recent chapter that she has read. Ask the standard questions: Who? What? When? Where? Why? How? Who are her favorite characters? Who is the hero, and who is the villain?

Over the semester, introduce a different element, and discuss it for a couple of weeks. To illustrate, weeks one and two could be devoted to "characters" while during weeks three and four you could introduce the element of "setting." Talk about major and minor characters. Have her describe their physical, mental, and spiritual attributes. Ask her to define what the various characters want. Approach setting like you would approach a piece of art. Look for the artist's intentions in using descriptive language to convey a particular mood.

Explain in weeks five and six how plot is the story line that runs from the (1) exposition in the beginning to the (2) rising action that culminates in the (3) climax which then is resolved in the (4) denouement or falling action to the (5) final conclusion. Have her condense the plot to one or two sentences. Show her how to look at the bare bones of the story by identifying each of the five phases of plot especially the climax when the main character's problem comes to a head.

During weeks seven and eight, discuss the idea of conflict and how the main character has a problem that he needs to overcome. Find all the conflicts in the story, and help her identify the major conflict that fuels the plot. Ask what the problems are, and if the solutions have not been revealed yet in her reading, have her predict how the author will solve.

Weeks nine and ten involve teaching the idea of theme. What are the main ideas of the story? Think in terms of abstract ideas like love, friendship, suffering, sacrifice, and freedom. Have her find examples of the themes in the body of the text. Discuss whether she agrees with the author's ideas or not.

Finally, you could show her various literary devices during weeks eleven and twelve like simile, metaphor, alliteration, and repetition. You might have to read the book with her (or skim it quickly if you don't have time) to find examples especially since you are much more familiar with these devices than she.

Each of these teaching concepts could be staggered over a much longer period of time (say an academic year, or even several years) depending on how deep you want to go with them. Decide if your purpose is to introduce her to the elements of fiction with a plan to examine them in detail as she gets older, or whether your purpose is to spend more time on each element now. Character and setting are the easiest elements to grasp, so if you want to slow the process down and spend more time on a concept, start with these two elements of fiction.

5. Assign her weekly writing from her literature reading.

She is the perfect age to begin expository writing especially since she enjoys reading narratives. Teach her how to structure a simple one-idea paragraph with a topic sentence and supporting sentences. Have her write one paragraph a week on the fictional element that you are currently discussing.

Since she enjoys reading about animals, assume for illustration purposes that she is reading *The Yearling* by Marjorie Rawlings. Here are some ideas for writing about the elements:

Characters:
Jody, Pa, Ma, the crippled boy Fodderwing, the fawn

Setting:
The woods of Florida, United States Reconstruction (post Civil War)

Plot:
Jody wants a pet, Ma says they can't afford one, he finds Flag, and fawn eats too much

Conflict:
Jody runs away to avoid decision about the fawn; faces own hunger; decides

Themes:
Love, grief, hardship, coming-of-age, responsibility, relationships

Let her come up with the single idea during your discussions and help her key word outline (three words per line) the idea then write her double-spaced draft from the outline. When she is ready, teach her how to add the stylistic dress-ups that you are teaching her older brother. Show her how

207

to end the paragraph with a few dramatic words that she can then echo in the title that she gives her essay. For instance, if her paragraph is on the theme of hunger, she can include some thought about hunger in the last sentence that is reflected in the title like this:

"Jody's growling, aching belly taught him the reality of hunger."

The "clincher" title could be "A Growling, Aching Belly" or "The Reality of Hunger" or a phrase that echoes these last words like "An Empty Stomach."

6. Purchase a sketchbook for her nature journal.

She loves the outdoors and nature, so give her a sketchbook and some colored pencils, and have her draw what she sees. Find an illustrated life science encyclopedia that she can consult after she has discovered a new creature (butterfly, ants, grasshoppers, birds) and read further. Use that particular creature as a springboard for finding lots of library books on the subject.

You can structure her nature study spontaneously by random field trips and walks, or you can plan thematic studies according to her interests and the opportunities in your area. Horses are a favorite animal, so take her to a local stable and let her draw the horses. Or perhaps there is a zoo or a working farm close by that you could visit to study the feline or the bovine family.

If you do a thematic unit, make sure that she notices the differences and similarities between the related animals of that unit. For example, there are lots of cats in the feline family, so how are they alike and how are they different?

7. Resume her math coursework.

Now that you have had a nice sabbatical from regular math, you might want to consider switching to a different math curriculum. *Saxon* math texts are excellent. Since you are not exactly sure how far behind she is for her age, search online for their 18 page PDF placement tests and have her take the primary grades exam. This will take some time on your part, so budget accordingly. You will follow the script and assign points for whether she understands the math concept or not. They provide templates and worksheets for all of the questions, so all you have to do is print out the assessment and assemble the manipulative aids.

Depending upon her total score, *Saxon* will recommend the exact text you should purchase. If you want to introduce math games on Fridays, that might be fun for your eleven, nine, and six year olds.

8. Ask her to choose some short stories about animals to memorize and recite.

Most children's illustrated picture books are short enough to provide good memorization material. Select some narratives from the library (perhaps the ones that she is already reading to little sis), and have her memorize the text. Tell her to pretend that she is a mom with a group of little children gathered around her knees eagerly waiting to hear her story. Have her practice reading it out loud with appropriate pacing, pitch, and pronunciation. If she thinks of the story as one dramatic unit, she might be able to create a mood that really compels the listeners. Give her a deadline for each story, and designate one week night or weekend day as performance time. Gather the entire family around, and let her entertain them with her talent.

Alice's Weekly Plan

- Pick out three illustrated books, and read to Teresa (weekly)
- Read with Mom (daily)
- Copy and correct the paragraph that Jack reads (weekly)
- Replace grammar parts of speech in dictation paragraph (weekly)
- Read at bedtime (daily)
- Write about one element of fiction from your literature (once a week)
- Sketch your observations while on field trips (weekly)
- Complete math lessons with Mom (weekly)

Progress Report

Sometime around the end of the semester, take an inventory with Alice of her progress. Ask her what she has and has not enjoyed about the past few weeks. If there were steps that did not work for Alice, eliminate them from the next semester and come up with an alternative plan.

Pull all of her work and take a big picture look at whether her skills have improved especially in grammar, the elements of fiction, writing simple sentences, and math. Keep working on those areas that need improvement.

Chapter 51
A Girly Girl

This six year old little princess, Teresa, describes herself as a "girly girl." Her favorite color is purple which, of course, is the color of royalty. Not surprisingly, she loves to play dress up in her red princess gown and her ballet costume. She loves to dance, draw, and read books about princesses and horses. Playing with Barbie dolls is another pastime. But she is not just an inside girl…she loves being outside and can distinguish a cowbird on a cedar with her acute powers of observation! Teresa is full of energy and always has something funny to say.

Mastery Status

Teresa almost knows the entire lowercase alphabet, with the exception of a few letters. She sings the ABC song close to perfection. The majority of her time over the next semester will be spent working on reading and thinking skills with a minimal amount of time spent on the third skill, speech.

Teresa's semester priorities:

READING SKILLS

How to read
How to write

THINKING SKILLS

How to arrange data according to systems
How to solve problems

SPEAKING SKILLS

How to have conversations
How to give a speech

Action Steps

1. Read to her daily.

Her older sister will be reading to her three times a week, so Mom and Dad can take the other two days to read colorful picture books to her while cuddled up together on the couch, in bed, at the kitchen table, or on the back porch. Give big sister Monday, Wednesday, and Friday as her reading days so that every other day, she is hearing an adult read. Since she loves princesses and ballet, select illustrated stories that engage her interests.

Use your index finger to show her how the text moves from left to right. Frequently point out simple words and say:

> "Do you see this word? This is the word for 'cat.' Cat is
> spelled 'c-a-t.' Can you spell cat? Use your fingers to
> point out each letter as you say it."

Start by pointing out short, three letter words of the same phonetic pattern (like cap, nap, rap, sap). Use lots of feeling when you read. Pause at commas. Raise and lower your voice for questions, exclamations, and commands.

2. Help her create her own alphabet book.

The ABC song is clear with the exception of the letters '-j, -k, and -z.' Teach her the names of the letters along with the sound. Describe the shapes as you write each letter for her. For instance, if you are teaching the letter 'j,' you could say:

> "To make the lowercase letter '-j,' put your pencil tip on the dotted line (if you are using ruled handwriting paper). Draw a straight line down from the dotted line past the bottom line then curl your '-j' to the left like a fishhook."

Spend the next few weeks building an ABC book by working on one or two letters a week.

Purchase a sketchbook, bind 30 pages at the local copy shop, or create your own book. Since you are so creative with digital scrap booking, and she has artistic abilities, show her how to decorate her ABC book. To create your own ABC book, use a three ring hole punch on two pieces of colorful tag board (the front and back covers) and lace the binding with ribbon, or glue scrapbook paper to the front cover of a purchased sketchbook. You could even use scrapbook letters in her book if you want, but be sure to have her copy her own letters on the page, too.

As you work on a letter, have her add the letter to her ABC book. Add the lowercase letters to the left page of a two page spread, and leave the right page blank. When she has learned her lowercase, you'll come back and add the uppercase letter on the right side. Let her practice making her letters after you show her how. Write the letter on the top of the page then let her copy it a few times. Use half of the page for the letter writing and the other half for her illustrations.

Since she loves drawing, let her illustrate her personal ABC book. After she writes her letter on the blank page, have her draw and color pictures that begin with the letter. Keep doing this until she fills the book with all 26 lowercase letters then teach her the uppercase letters and do the same thing with the ABC book.

You could also use this opportunity to teach her about the components of books like the title page (add one to her book with her name on it as the author), the table of contents (add the page numbers as a way of counting), and put page numbers on the bottom of all the pages just like a real story book.

3. Play sight word games with her.

The three sight word lists (appendix) contain the 300 most common words that will appear in her reading materials for the next few years. You can help her master these sight words in many different ways. You could show her the first list and have her read the ones that she knows; you'll cross them off as she gets them correct.

You could create a bingo game with the sight words by grouping those that look similar like 'her, here, him, his, how, had, have, and has.' There are websites that allow you to create free bingo games of many sizes, or since she is artistic, help her set up the bingo cards, decorate the borders, and even write the selected words in the rows.

Another idea for learning sight words while playing games is using the Scrabble letters to form the words. You can form the words then ask her what they say, or you can give her the letter tiles and let her spell the word as you say it. Magnetic letters also work well for this activity.

When you see a sight word in the text that you are reading, be sure to point it out to her. If you see one on the page, you could tell her that you see a sight word, and ask her if she can find it.

4. Teach her how to build words with the phonetic blends.

When she knows most of her letters and a growing list of sight words, it is time to start building words. Work with one root at a time. Look for "Phonetic Roots" in the appendix of this book.

For instance the two letters 'a' and 'n' when put together make the sound 'an.' All you have to do is add a consonant at the beginning to make different words. Get a blank piece of paper. Write the letter combination 'an' in a vertical column down the paper several times. Then write all the consonants that you can think of that would make a word with 'an' across the top of the page. Give her a pencil, and have her build her own words by adding a new consonant to each line of '-an.' Let her pronounce each new word. Have her show Dad when he gets home what she is learning about building new words.

If she enjoyed making her own ABC book, you could create another book for her new nouns and verbs. Have her count how many words she can create on each page.

5. Designate bedtime as personal reading time.

When you visit the library each week, encourage her to pick out as many picture books as she wants for her bedtime "reading." Put a purple crate or bookshelf by her bed for her library books. Make this a pleasant nightly ritual (of about 30 minutes) before you turn the lights out. If she wants to read to little brothers, let them all pile up on the bed and let her explain the story through pictures. She'll feel more grown up and responsible while getting them excited about learning to read.

6. Increase her familiarity with numbers.

She counts to sixteen and backwards from ten to one with no problem. Gradually introduce each new set of ten working your way up to one hundred. Show her that all numbers, no matter how big, are only put together with the numbers 0-9. Write the numbers 1 through 10 on a piece of paper, and keep adding tens (11-20; 21-30; etc.) under the prior set of ten like this:

1	2	3	4	5	6	7	8	9	10
11	12	13	14	15	16	17	18	19	20

Take advantage of opportunities to count. When you are at the grocery, have her count the apples, or when you are traveling back and forth between houses, have her count all the blue cars. Unless you sense differently, a formal math text is not necessary yet. Use manipulative objects around the house and yard to make adding and subtracting concrete and less abstract.

7. Use her outdoor play time for building analytical skills.

She loves to play outside, so allow as much as possible. As you are lounging, hiking, swimming, or riding bikes together, have conversations about her surroundings. Casually ask her to describe what she is seeing. How is the cowbird on the cedar different from the blue jay in the cherry tree? Sometimes ask her how the things that she is seeing are the same. If you see patterns in nature like the patterns on the back of leaves, point them out to her. Teach her to use all five of her senses to discover and describe the world around her.

8. Suggest that she memorize and recite a few good jokes.

Since she is so quick-witted and enjoys humor, help her find some goofy jokes to memorize and share with her family members. Sometimes she said she makes up her own jokes, so let her draw her own three panel cartoons for her original ideas. When you arrange a family recitation night, have her contribute by telling jokes. Her little brothers will giggle and guffaw with glee!

Teresa's Weekly Plan

- Read with Mom (daily)

- Create your own ABC book (weekly)

- Play word games with Mom (weekly)

- Build new words with Mom (weekly)

- Memorize some good jokes to recite (occasionally)

- Read at bedtime (daily)

Progress Report

Sometime around the end of the semester, take an inventory of Teresa's progress. How far has she advanced in learning her lower and uppercase alphabet? Is she starting to recognize certain simple words in the text? Can she read any words in her picture books out loud? How high can she count? Keep reading and working on those areas that need improvement.

Chapter 52
Action Steps for David and Ruth

Four strategic plans represent lots of information to digest, so I prepared a comprehensive "to-do" list for David and Ruth. In this list, I have taken the action steps for all four children and segregated these steps into (a) one-time tasks like purchase books and (b) recurring tasks like weekly reading.

Once David and Ruth a have had a chance to read the four plans, they can decide what suggestions they will implement and allocate the work amongst themselves. There are certain teaching goals that David is best equipped to handle while other teaching goals are clearly in Ruth's domain.

Preliminary ONE-TIME Action Steps

- ❑ Purchase a typing text for Jack
- ❑ Purchase a Kay Arthur *Precepts* beginner's Bible study for Jack
- ❑ Purchase voice recorder for Todd, or customize voice recognition software
- ❑ Purchase headset with microphone for Todd
- ❑ Purchase index cards and bell for Todd
- ❑ Purchase *Audio Memory's* "Grammar Songs" for Todd
- ❑ Purchase appropriate *Saxon* math for Todd and Alice
- ❑ Purchase a sketchbook for Alice
- ❑ Investigate possible robotics competitions for Jack
- ❑ Create a narration page for Todd (2/3 blank; 1/3 lined)
- ❑ Download the *Saxon* elementary placement test for Todd and Alice
- ❑ Record a story about King Arthur for Todd to memorize
- ❑ Show Alice how to substitute grammar in her dictation paragraph
- ❑ Create an alphabet book for Teresa
- ❑ Create sight word bingo or Scrabble for Teresa
- ❑ Teach Jack, Todd, and Alice how to key word outline
- ❑ Teach Jack, Todd, and Alice how to draft a one-idea paragraph
- ❑ Teach Jack how to add all six stylistic dress-ups
- ❑ Teach Jack, Todd, and Alice how to perform a lab using the scientific method
- ❑ Teach Jack how to write claims for his inventions

Third Family

* * * * *

RECURRING Action Steps

With your 13 year old:

- Find some history documentaries for Jack and David to watch together
- Assign a few scientific discoveries for Jack to memorize and recite

With your 11 year old:

- Read to Todd (daily)
- Copy down two to three sentences from Todd's narration (weekly)
- Teach phonics to Todd (weekly)
- Create phonics bingo game, word wall, and bell game cards for Todd (weekly)
- Discuss Todd's literature "reading" books on tape (weekly)
- Teach one element of fiction to Todd (once a week)

With your 9 year old:

- Read to Alice (daily)
- Teach grammar parts of speech to Alice (one a week)
- Discuss Alice's literature reading (weekly)
- Teach one element of fiction to Alice (once a week)

With your 6 year old:

- Read to Teresa (daily)
- Work on Teresa's ABC book (weekly)
- Play sight word games with Teresa (weekly)
- Teach Teresa how to build new words (weekly)
- Work with Teresa on her numbers (weekly)

With all the kids:

- Take the kids to the library (once a week)
- Take the kids on a field trip (weekly)

Fourth Family

&

Henry, Jean, and Twin Sons

Chapter 53
Software Engineer Times Two

What is the likelihood of meeting your future husband, an American civilian, overseas while you are on a military tour of duty? While serving in the U. S. Air Force, Jean, a computer software engineer, met Henry, also a computer engineer, while he was working as a support contractor at the Air Force Simulation Center in Germany. Henry's contract was over before Jean's commission expired, so he headed home to resume his work in the States. Not long after that, she took an engineering position with the same multinational company where Henry worked, and they were married and began their family.

High energy fraternal twin sons, ages 10 years old, require their parents' total attention! Living in the American West, this family takes full advantage of the outdoors by snowboarding, dirt biking, camping, and fishing. The boys' most recent nature project involved collecting frogs, crickets, and pond water for fun. Not surprisingly since their parents are techies, the boys also really enjoy computer games.

Two years ago, Jean began to notice that one of her sons was struggling in the local public school, so she pulled both boys out of the system and began to home school them while she continued to work full-time. Jean comes from a family of teachers, including her mom, so the idea of home schooling was not overwhelming, and she tackled the task with gusto. Now that she is no longer working, she devotes her entire concentration to managing the boys' education.

In a brief amount of time, Jean has cultivated a great support network both in her local neighborhood and on a few Yahoo Groups. Her quick wit and friendly, outgoing personality make her the perfect friend as she encourages other home school moms. She and the boys are fortunate to participate in a weekly recreational play group of like-minded families.

Spend a few minutes getting to know her better by reading her responses to my questions about home schooling before you meet her son, Jason, and read his strategic semester plan.

When were you first introduced to the idea of home schooling?

I first heard about it in 2005 when a co-worker mentioned that his wife was home schooling their children. I had been struggling to make public school work for my kids at that time, and I was also struggling to balance work with their school. I became extremely interested and bombarded my co-worker with questions about how to do it, what it takes, where to get curriculum, and similar questions. I knew at that point that somehow I had to restructure our life in order to make it happen.

Why did you decide to teach your kids at home?

Because working with the public school in order to bend it to best accommodate Jason and his difficulties was taking as much time and was more frustrating than if I taught the boys myself! I pulled my other son out, too, because I wanted them to both have the same environment. I like being in control of their education and setting our own pace and course.

How long have you been home schooling?

This will be our third year.

What moments related to home schooling have brought you the greatest joy?

These moments bring joy: little breakthroughs in understanding, the blossoming of Jason as a wonderful person to be around, and seeing my other son excel at new lessons.

What moments related to home schooling have brought you the most frustration?

The boys' reluctance to put forth any real effort and to take schooling more seriously frustrates me. I know – they're still young. Every morning there are groans when they have to do work, but once we get going, they are usually OK.

How organized would you say your home school is?

We are fairly loose and relaxed.

How structured is your typical day?

> We are not what I would consider "structured." However, we do have a list of subjects that I like to accomplish for each day of the week. I have that "schedule" posted on a wall for the boys' reference. Each day is different and allows for co-op, Park Day, and field trips. We cover Literature (read-aloud books), Silent Reading, Writing, Spelling, Math, Science, History, and Piano. We have occasional short-term subjects like Cursive Writing and *Brainware Safari* (for cognitive thinking skills), which usually only last 10-12 weeks when we do them.

Do you take breaks throughout the calendar year?

> We mostly follow a 3-month-on, 1-month-off kind of schedule. We take other breaks when the opportunity arises. This kind of schedule loosely aligns with our local public school's year-round schedule. This is so that my other son has an easier time getting together with his public school friend.

Do you have a dedicated room just for school?

> No, mostly we use the family room for sitting together and reading or working on small white boards, or the floor for games, and the dining room for some of the seat work.

What general areas do you feel qualified to teach?

> Math is my forte, but I have a strong background in literature and writing as well. I love science and history and do well teaching these. I played piano most of my teen years, but I am extremely rusty as an adult.

Are there any areas of study in which you feel inadequate?

> Logic (when we get to it) and literary analysis at the intermediate/middle school level.

Are there other things that you want to teach them that you haven't had time to do yet?

> Yes, but mostly because they aren't quite ready yet. For instance, full grammar, Greek/Latin roots, logic, and Spanish.

223

What is your biggest concern or question about giving your kids a classical education?

I am concerned about how long it will take them to realize how important their work is and start to take more of an interest in their own education. I know that this is just a maturity issue, and that it probably won't happen this year either, but sometimes it is hard to believe that they will "turn the corner" as they mature and become more serious about learning. So my fear is that even by 14 or 15 years old, they still won't be interested. I have seen this happen with other teenagers, including my stepsons. However, I have to realize that I can't make comparisons like these since each child is raised in an entirely different environment. I figure by the time they are approaching high school age, I will have taught them the three skills of the trivium and that they will pretty much have them mastered, but I don't know if they will ever be ready for the next step. I need to have faith that what we are doing now is going to prepare them well for when nature takes its course, and they start to mature. Some days it's just hard to see that happening when they are such "kids" now, only interested in play, play, play!

Chapter 54
Constantly Spinning Plot Lines

Imagination fuels this budding writer! Ten year old Jason is a master storyteller weaving details of brave heroes, mythical creatures, epic battles, and dangerous weapons. Sometimes his ideas come in dreams, and occasionally he spins a plot line from a movie, video game, or book. In addition to his own alter-ego, Jason uses his twin brother and a friend as the inspiration for the good guys who consistently crush evil until the next episode when the threat resurfaces. He enjoys learning about "back-then battles" which is what he calls ancient and medieval military history. Writing is his favorite academic pursuit. His ideas come faster than he is able to type or write, so Mom helps capture his creativity by scribing as he dictates.

When Jason was attending public school, Jean noticed that he seemed overly anxious and inattentive. Naturally concerned, Jean arranged for Jason to see a psychologist who ran a complete battery of tests to determine a baseline for improvement. The tests revealed mild auditory, visual, and language processing issues which are manifested when Jason misplaces adjectives in his speech or says "pick a number from 10 to 1" instead of "from 1 to 10." Additionally, he has trouble writing what he is thinking which could be caused by neurological or fine motor delays. Finally, he was diagnosed with sequential and working memory deficits. Relief flooded over Jean as the doctor confirmed what she intuitively knew, and she now structures Jason's learning experiences to address these developmental obstacles.

One other physical issue has been successfully remedied. Jason was feeling depressed, angry, and antisocial (perhaps due to his body's inability to keep up with his quick mind), so he is currently taking medication to stabilize his moods. Remarkable improvement has resulted in a happier disposition and an increased desire to spend time with friends.

Mastery Status

An engaging and smart boy, Jason has an extensive vocabulary for his age, and he regularly uses sophisticated syntax like clausal opening phrases and compound-complex sentences in his conversations. When chatting, he uses accurate tense and proper subject-verb placement. Like any other ten year old, he has command of the language when he speaks, but he has trouble translating his thoughts correctly on paper. This is simply a matter of teaching him the rules of spelling, punctuation, and grammar. For this reason, he needs to spend a majority of the semester working on application of language rules (skill one).

Games will play a role in improving his thinking skills (skill two) as will learning how to predict outcomes by performing experiments using the scientific method. Finally, he will use his active imagination to learn how to deliver interpretive speeches and write basic one topic paragraphs (skill three).

Jason's semester priorities:

READING SKILLS

How to read
How to spell
How to write
How to punctuate and capitalize
How to use proper grammar

THINKING SKILLS

How to arrange data according to systems
How to solve problems
How to use the scientific method

SPEAKING SKILLS

How to write a paragraph
How to give a speech

Action Steps

1. Share the responsibility for reading to him every day.

You are giving him such an incredible gift by reading to him every day! Studies show that kids whose parents invest in daily reading time have a significantly higher vocabulary, increased attention span, and a lifelong interest in books. The only thing better for Jason than having Mom read to him would be having Dad read to him. Dad is his male role model, and Jason will naturally pattern his own adult life based upon what he sees his Dad doing now. If Dad invested even twenty minutes a week in read aloud time, Jason would learn that reading is not just for women and children; therefore, he would be more likely to make reading a lifelong habit into adulthood. Plus, that special bond between father and sons will strengthen as fond memories are created.

As you read, pause occasionally and ask Jason to predict what will happen next. Have him narrate the main points of the plot after you finish a chapter. Ask him who his favorite characters were and what he liked and disliked about the story. If you learn to ask who, what, when, where, how, and why questions each time that you read to him, you really don't need to purchase special curricula for teaching classic literature. Formal literary analysis can wait until the teenage years.

Engage his critical thinking skills while you read, too. Ask him to compare characters, contrast settings, and describe plot lines. Have him find similarities and differences. Help him identify the main problem in the story, and ask him how he would solve it if he were the author.

2. Have him read one short selection out loud every day to you.

Jason needs to see the written word in order to improve his spelling and punctuation skills. This may not be a popular action step, but it is critical to his improvement in language skills. When he read the sample excerpts for me, he was eager to read them all, even the most difficult one (he likes a challenge), but he quickly skipped over unfamiliar words instead of trying to sound them out. Have him read every word, and show him how to sound out the syllables. If you are there with him, you can correct his pronunciation on the spot and provide immediate feedback. As he improves in his pronunciation, show him how to read with feeling. Tell him to pretend that he is an actor in a movie.

Once a week, have him also say the punctuation marks as he reads. (If he balks, tell him that when he publishes his first book for sale, his publisher will have him read all the punctuation marks, so he might as well start practicing now.) He already uses punctuation in his own writing, so all he needs is a little practice seeing proper usage so that he will begin to do the same when he writes. Use this weekly ritual to teach one usage rule like how to punctuate two complete thoughts or how to contract two words using an apostrophe.

As for the reading selection, look for topics that interest him like medieval history or fantasy. Choose books with challenging vocabulary. He knows how to spell the basic words, but multi-syllable words like "previously" still give him trouble. You could have him read one or two paragraphs a day from a fiction chapter book or from his nonfiction medieval history text. Kids who frequently read good literature tend to be better spellers than those who complete spelling workbooks.

3. Teach grammar rules in the context of his daily reading.

Instead of purchasing an official grammar program, use his daily readings to teach grammar concepts. Spend several weeks on each of the eight parts of speech. Start with nouns. Make a copy of Monday's paragraph and highlight all the common and proper nouns. Tell him that a noun is a person, place, or thing. Ask him to identify all the nouns in the room. When you think he understands the concept, give him the highlighter so that he can find all the nouns. If you want to vary the exercise, give him the copy of the paragraph and have him substitute all the nouns. If he likes to draw, let him draw the nouns. Or set the timer and send him on a scavenger hunt to find nouns.

Once he masters nouns, move on to pronouns and adjectives. Have him create adjective and noun combinations. After that, teach him verbs in context of his reading selections then adverbs. Stick to the eight parts of speech for now. You've got plenty of time to cover the more advanced grammar concepts like gerunds and participles over the next two or three years.

4. Purchase the grammar songs CD by *Audio Memory*.

My kids still sing these songs when they want to recall a grammar rule! Coordinate the songs with the particular grammar rule that you are teaching that week. Play them in the car or in the house. Let him dance if he wants to while he sings!

5. Teach spelling rules in the context of composition assignments.

Since you are reading to him daily, he has many opportunities to see how common words are spelled. Use his composition assignments as a platform for teaching spelling rules in context. Spelling workbooks are easier on the parents, but the child doesn't really benefit from the drill. What if he already knows how to spell 80% of that lesson's words? He has spent valuable time doing busy work just to learn 2 out of 10 words.

My entire family loved Jason's original composition, "Slayer's Battle for Freedom." In fact, laughter gripped each one of us when we encountered the witty name of his villain! His vivid language reflects a passion for action, adventure, and suspense. Many people want to write but fail for lack of ideas. Jason has enormous potential as a writer because he is brimming with creative ideas. Now all he needs to perfect is the form to go with his substance.

I understand why you are scribing for him, but you miss an opportunity to teach spelling rules when you type the words for him. For example, there were several misspelled words in his draft of "Slayer's Battle." He needs to find his own errors in his writing and correct them in order to see a tangible purpose for correct spelling. Teach him about editors and proofreading by circling his misspelled words and having him correct them in the next draft. Or tell him how many errors there were, and let him find them all.

If he doesn't know the difference between the homonyms "there, their, and they're," use his writing as a chance to explain when to use each form of the word. Look at his errors, and see if there is a pattern. If you are concerned about his long-term memory, play spelling games to give him repetitive practice with particularly tricky words.

6. Continue using your current math program.

It sounds like you are happy with his progress in learning mathematics, so there is no need to make a change. Since the program is not grade specific, you might want to have him take the free online math placement text that *Saxon Publishers* offers just to get a feel for how he compares with his peers. He might be like his parents and have a knack for math and engineering.

Leave time in the schedule for fun learning. Games, puzzles, riddles, and mysteries are equally effective thinking tools. If the drill of the math text is wearing him down, put it away, and pull out an unexpected puzzle treat.

7. Do a weekly experiment using the scientific method.

He likes earth and space science, and he likes to collect little critters like frogs, so take advantage of his interests by performing experiments once a week. Janice van Cleave has written a series of paperbacks containing fun experiments with easily obtained materials. Tell him how every scientist comes up with an informed guess (hypothesis) which he then tests by making predictions and seeing if they are accurate or not. He's probably not ready for the detailed steps of documenting an experiment, but he is ready for this mantra: "Observe. Predict. Conclude."

8. Keep teaching stylistic elements with IEW materials.

Use *Institute for Excellence in Writing* (IEW) for teaching technique once a week. Have him practice keyword outlining from nonfiction texts, turn the text over, then let him narrate what he's going to write from the outline. Work on all six dress-ups until he has mastered them. Rushing on to decorations, triples, and advanced techniques is not necessary. He has at least eight more years to write with you, so there is plenty of time to learn the other stylistic techniques in the future.

9. Teach him how to write a basic, one idea paragraph.

Once you are happy with his ability to write from someone else's text, teach him about the paragraph. Theoretically, the paragraphs that he has been "rewriting" are well written with one main thought per paragraph. Show him what a topic sentence looks like and how the rest of the sentences support that main thought. Once a week, give him a topic and ask him to come up with three supporting points for that topic.

For example, let's say you gave him the topic "water pistols." In thinking of supporting points, he might describe (1) the various sizes of the toy, (2) the games you could play with the toy, and (3) places where you can find the toy. Now let him write his main point: "water pistols are the perfect summer toy." Show him how to write that point first then create supporting sentences for the other three sub points. Tell him that later he will learn to expand his writing to include a separate paragraph for point 1 – sizes, point 2 – games, and point 3 – places.

Whatever you do, don't limit his writing to the *IEW* nonfiction texts. He has the gift of storytelling, and you need to nurture that creativity by letting him write from his own mind. You can teach the one idea paragraph with fiction, too. Give him a character, setting, or plot as the main idea, and let him come up with the three supporting points. This exercise will also prepare him for original speeches in the future.

10. Require one or two interpretive speeches this semester.

Of all the different type of speeches, Jason is particularly suited to interpretive speeches because of his storytelling ability and humor. You can use a children's story book, a script, or a section of a chapter book as long as it has lots of dialogue. Shoot for a three minute speech which is about three paragraphs. You may have to cut a longer piece.

In this exercise, he reads the piece of literature and acts out all the characters without props or costumes. He can adopt a different voice and mannerisms for each character. Memorization will make the delivery even better, so let him work on it for a few weeks before presenting it to Dad and brother. Narration like "he said" should be omitted. To help him memorize the speech, have him record it (tape recorder or laptop) by reading it out loud all the way through then listening to it over and over until he has it memorized.

Jason's Weekly Plan

- Read one to three paragraphs out loud to Mom (daily)
- Learn to sing the grammar songs from memory
- Correct your spelling errors in your writing (as you find them)
- Continue with your math lessons (weekly)
- Do one experiment a week
- Write every week and add your stylistic dress ups
- Memorize one fun speech and give it to your family

Progress Report

Sometime around the end of the semester, take an inventory with Jason of his progress. Ask him what he has and has not enjoyed about the past few weeks. If there were steps that did not work for Jason, eliminate them from the next semester and come up with an alternative plan.

Pull all of his work and take a big picture look at whether his skills have improved especially in spelling, punctuation, and capitalization. Keep working on those areas that need improvement.

Chapter 55
Action Steps for Henry and Jean

As I did for the other parents, I have taken Jason's action steps and segregated them into (a) one-time tasks like purchase books and (b) recurring tasks like weekly reading.

Once Henry and Jean have had a few weeks to think about the suggested plan, they can decide what ideas they will implement and allocate the work amongst themselves. There are certain teaching goals that Henry is best equipped to handle while other teaching goals are clearly in Jean's domain.

Preliminary ONE-TIME Action Steps

☐ Purchase "Grammar Songs" CD from *Audio Memory*
☐ Have him take the *Saxon Publishers* online math assessment
☐ Find one piece of literature that he can memorize for the interpretive speech.

* * * * *

RECURRING Action Steps

- Read good literature to him every day
- Correct his pronunciation as you hear mistakes
- Find his spelling errors in his compositions
- Play thinking games with him once a week
- Pull together the supplies for one experiment a week

- Teach him all six writing dress-ups
- Teach him how to write a one idea paragraph
- Teach him to sound out the syllables of unfamiliar words
- Teach one punctuation usage rule a week
- Teach the eight parts of speech

Fifth Family

&

Mark, Julia, One Son, and One Daughter

Chapter 56
Quality Trumps Quantity

Fiercely committed to quality family time, Mark and Julia take turns driving over 180 miles every weekend to keep their family steadfast and orbiting together! As founding member of a management-consulting firm that assists clients in identifying and investigating potential acquisitions, Mark is obligated to travel five days a week. Some Friday nights, Mark drives home to his wife, Julia, and their two children, Austin (16 years old) and Marie (12 years old) while other Friday nights, Julia and the kids drive to Mark's "home away from home" for a long weekend. This family knows how important genuine quality is over careless quantity, and they strive to make every moment count.

Because Julia has a very positive attitude about travel, the kids enjoy the adventure and regularly complete their academic assignments in the car. Wireless internet access makes researching debate theory in the car a breeze. Mark jokingly tells Julia that "you do anything but home school because you are never home!"

Armed with an economics undergraduate degree and years of experience, this driven professional is an expert at seeing the strategic big picture while sifting through financial and operations data. He loves the challenge of turning around a failing company, and he never leaves a task undone. Competitive by nature, Mark eagerly relishes the race to finish any task in the most efficient way possible. Julia calls her energetic husband a sprinter with excellence as his goal.

Mark expects his wife and children to pursue excellence, as well. Looking to the data, he constantly encourages improvements in the home school. Mark grew up in a little southern town populated almost exclusively by relatives, so his public school experience was a delightful family affair with cousins for classmates.

Contrary to Mark's fun, Julia found public school so stifling that she accelerated her class load so that she could graduate a year early and escape the boredom. Consequently, when Julia approached Mark about home schooling, he was initially amused but dubious about the proposal, never expecting her to go all the way through high school graduation.

Now Mark concedes that home schooling has been a success as he sees how happy and well-balanced his children have become.

Despite Julia's travel schedule, she practices hospitality wherever she finds herself. Whether in a restaurant with friends or in a home school club meeting, Julia is extravagantly generous with her time and resources. Conversation with friends and family is a favorite pastime, but she doesn't dominate by chattering away; rather, she is a careful listener who offers wise counsel when asked. Her kids adore her and sincerely enjoy time in her presence. Spend a few minutes getting to know her better by reading her responses to my questions about home schooling before you meet her daughter, Marie, and read her strategic semester plan for mastering the three skills of the classical trivium. Austin's strategic plan can be found in *Socratic Paideia: Dialogue Drives Instruction*, the sequel to this book.

When were you first introduced to the idea of home schooling?

> I had heard of it and already had this vague feeling "that sounds like where I belong in the education world," but the first actual family I knew to home school was a good friend and next door neighbor when Austin was about three years old. When I actually started home schooling a couple of years later, it was a very lonely experience and most people in my neighborhood couldn't understand why I wanted to spend my time doing that. It is especially comical now that two of my neighbor's children are home school students.

Why did you decide to teach your kids at home?

> The Bible calls us to raise our children up in the way of the Lord and to protect them. Given the lack of prayer, the illegal drugs even at the elementary level, violence, promotion of anti-Biblical principals (homosexual behavior, anti-family agendas), low academic offerings and standards in public or private schools these days, it does not appear possible to honor those commandments even in a superficial way much less in the spirit they are intended.

How long have you been home schooling?

> We've been home schooling for ten years.

What moments related to home schooling have brought you the greatest joy?

The greatest joy is just being with my children in a peaceful environment where we are free to exist in a caring, kind, loving, and serving relationship with one another. (Of course this utopia comes with the occasional sibling stuff, but it's just not that often. Most days are an absolute delight.) The most fun work I have ever done is participating with them as they learn to "ask, seek and knock" (on whatever the subject). I am very blessed to have two children who are healthy, bright, and willing to do their work so our frustrations are few.

What moments related to home schooling have brought you the most frustration?

Probably the biggest source of frustration for my kids is the fact that they want more contact with friends on a daily basis as opposed to the feast and famine. For instance, a week spent at a debate tournament will have to be balanced with two weeks of "get ahead" or "catch up" work without interruption of social gatherings other than regularly scheduled items like basketball, book club, and Rosebuds (monthly mother and daughter club). But in today's world of e-mail, chat for the older ones, texting, phones and such this is not even that big a deal.

How organized would you say your home school is?

I would go with a description of "organized chaos." To the outsider our comings and goings, lesson days versus "run around" days might appear to be disjointed, but when the steady progression and completion of all our subjects by year end (and that date varies!) is coupled with well above average results on annual standardized tests, I think we get an A in organization.

How structured is your typical day?

Fairly structured in the sense that everyone knows we attack school first with scheduled items (music lessons, sports, and art class) falling as they may. But, having said that, if an opportunity comes up, we can move all the home lessons to the evening or double up the next day. Opportunities come in various forms:

- another family asks you to participate in a special fieldtrip
- someone has "extra tickets"
- it's pouring rain and the schedule was go to the park
- it's snowing so we go sledding

Do you take breaks throughout the calendar year?

We started out following the public school schedule to avoid notice as much as possible with the exception of family vacations that have always been timed to miss the crowds. At this point following the public school calendar is not a consideration because it is too difficult to understand with all the half days, early summer start, and numerous teacher "in service" days. We generally take two days at Thanksgiving, two weeks for Christmas-New Year holiday, and a week of spring break along with the occasional Friday or Monday off for a long weekend. And, our school is closed on the birthdays of all students and teachers!

Do you have a dedicated room just for school?

Initially yes, we had a dedicated home school room painted, decked out with TV, VCR (before CD/DVD), book shelves, child-size table, sofa, and supplies galore ...the works! As the kids have passed elementary school, we moved upstairs which means my son is in the office, my daughter is on the sofa, and I am at the kitchen table. It's really 'go to where you are comfortable' and 'whoever gets the spot first.'

They still have desks (in an area off the kitchen), and there are supplies galore (instead of being housed in a big cabinet, they are organized in large canvas bags with the contents written on the outside and hanging on a freestanding coat rack for easy access), book shelves (a pie cabinet that doesn't look like a bookshelf...the things we've hidden in there!) So now the house and car are our dedicated home schooling areas.

What general areas do you feel qualified to teach?

Math, science, history, English (lit & grammar), and social studies are easy for me.

Are there any areas of study in which you feel inadequate?

Foreign language and maybe some higher level math make me feel inadequate.

Are there other things that you want to teach them that you haven't had time to do yet?

There are lots of "subjects to come" when the age and timing is right, but at this time it feels like we've made time for everything important.

What is your biggest concern or question about giving your kids a classical education?

My biggest question with breaking from the pack (public and private school ways) is this: will it be difficult later for children not raised in the pack to navigate and live around the pack? But, as the years go by and the kids appear to be successfully meeting life's challenges, this is less and less of a concern. Secondly, since the task of selecting resource material is so huge by saying "we are going to study this to the exclusion of studying that", am I able to include all the best content within a subject?

* * * * *

Mark and Julia's oldest child, Austin (16) is pursuing high school level studies, and as such, his makeover is included in the sequel to this book, *Socratic Paideia: Dialogue Leads to Discipline*. Now meet their 12 year old daughter, Marie, and read her strategic semester plan.

Chapter 57
Caught up in a Great Adventure

Independent and self-motivated, twelve year old Marie is a young woman with a mind of her own: she knows who she is and what she wants! Does Marie have free time? No problem. She can always find a project and teach herself how to complete it. For example, Marie taught herself how to knit, crochet and cross stitch as well as how to make jewelry, origami, and papier-mâché. She's not timid about asking for help, though, and when she starts a project, she eagerly works until it is done. Once while on a family visit, Marie used her persuasive powers to convince her grandmother to teach her how to sew. Energized by the excitement, they stayed up late into the night until a lovely, feminine dress materialized.

Perhaps one reason Marie never lacks for a project is because she has a knack for coming up with great ideas. Extremely creative, she often thinks "outside of the box." She has a big heart and anticipates the needs of others by regularly surprising them with peanut butter toast, handmade bracelets, or cards. Servant leadership comes natural to Marie. Recently, she invited several girlfriends to join a book club, and every month, she publishes a pink and purple newsletter full of book reviews and contests. Her most significant idea to date is a mystery novel that she is drafting; not surprisingly, the plot line involves a young heroine, much like Marie, who is caught up in a great adventure.

Mastery Status

Marie is an extremely articulate young woman who knows how to populate an essay with memorable content, but her punctuation needs more work, especially if she plans to publish her mystery novel or write professional newsletters. When reading her compositions, you feel like you are having a face-to-face conversation because she adds lots of juicy details and asks leading questions. Literature, grammar, and writing are her favorite subjects, and with the exception of a few punctuation errors, she has substantially mastered language, the first road of the classical trivium. To capitalize on her natural ability to come up with great ideas, Marie needs to learn how to use associations to solve difficult logical puzzles, document nature observations, and analyze literature each of which will improve her thinking skills. As for the third road of the trivium, speech, Marie will focus on refining the one-idea paragraph and experimenting with interpretive speeches. This plan concentrates on the following skills:

Marie's semester priorities:

READING SKILLS

How to punctuate and capitalize

THINKING SKILLS

How to solve problems
How to analyze literature

SPEAKING SKILLS

How to write a paragraph
How to give a speech

Action Steps

1. Require that she use the "spell-check" tool in her word processing program.

Marie's writing sample indicates a good working knowledge of advanced grammar concepts like how write a clausal opener and how to punctuate an appositive, so I assume that missing punctuation (no comma before direct quotations and no comma before conjunctions) can be explained by a failure to read the document again one last time for errors. Since lack of knowledge doesn't appear to be the problem, commit to using the "spell-check" tool before turning in essays or publishing newsletters. Many people do not know that this tool not only checks English spelling but also highlights punctuation errors and sentence fragments while offering corrective suggestions.

2. Continue pre-algebra using the current math text.

Teaching Textbooks is tailored to meet the needs of independent, self-motivated students like Marie. Since she consistently receives high scores, there is no need to make any changes to her math schedule. If she is not already doing so, have her grade her own work and correct any errors. If she consistently scores 90% or above, consider dropping her required problem set by half as long as she maintains an A average. Although she performs well in math, it is not one of her favorite subjects, and there is no indication that she will pursue a mathematically heavy undergraduate degree program. Encourage regular math exercises for the purpose of developing thinking skills and problem solving.

3. Purchase a sketchbook for her nature observations.

Inductive reasoning skills (observe, interpret, and apply) start with close observation of the circumstances or facts. She loves to draw, so purchase an artist's sketchbook, a magnifying glass, and some colored pencils so that she can reproduce the plants that she is learning about in her botany text. Send her outside once a week to discover a new species. Have her look very closely. What does she see? She should draw all of the pertinent elements like roots, stems, leaves, flowers, fruit, and seeds. When she comes back in, have her try to locate the exact plant in a photographic reference book like the Audubon Society's field guides to North American trees or wildflowers. For even more detail, look for a reference guide specific to your state. When she travels, she can take her sketchbook and expand her collection of drawings to include other areas of the country.

4. Assign a seasonal garden project.

Over time, Marie will observe plant species that do well in her region of the country. She can now interpret the results of her findings and apply her knowledge by planning, planting, and tending her own garden. Designate a section of the yard for a garden. The U.S. Department of Agriculture has labeled your area of the country zone 5A (northern and central Midwest), and you can easily search online or talk to your local nursery about which plants will thrive in your home town. Have her measure the plot and research the plants based on hardiness, moisture and light requirements, height, and color. Once she has an idea of what she wants to plant, let her draw out the garden to scale. Take the sketch to the nursery, and select the plants. As the garden matures, have her record her observations of the progress on a weekly basis in a separate garden log. Encourage her to quantify her findings using actual measurements and descriptions. Learning how to make predictions as the season proceeds is also a good way to improve inductive thinking skills.

5.   Assign selected biographies and autobiographies for her history reading.

Marie loves to read about people, so take advantage of her interests, and let her compile her own history reading program based on biographies and autobiographies.   Let her select a narrow window of history for her semester focus. She may enjoy selecting a particular country, gender, or chronological period for her reading.   A helpful reference guide to biographies would point to the books she wants to find. For instance, let's say she wants to narrow her reading to American Women. *Notable Women in American History,* available at Amazon, provides 500 brief summaries of famous American women along with bibliographies of all biographies written about each woman. She could quickly find her preferred time period (say colonial) and then browse the summaries to select a candidate. Next, she could see which biography or autobiography she wants to order or find at the library.

Biographies are great tools for absorbing historical context without having to read a dry history survey. There is plenty of time for large scale surveys later after she masters the three skills of the trivium.   Narrative histories reinforce inductive thinking skills by teaching the reader to observe, interpret, and apply the facts and lessons of history to their own culture and circumstances.

6. Purchase *Mindbenders* software for sharpening her deductive thinking skills.

Since this is her first year as a novice debater, this is the perfect time to introduce *Mindbenders* software from *Critical Thinking Press*. Each puzzle provides clues that connect people, places, and things.   Marie will eliminate the most obvious associations first with her computer mouse, and then she will move on to the less obvious associations until she has solved the puzzle. The puzzles progress in difficulty, and with nearly 120 puzzles to solve, she will greatly improve her deductive thinking skills.

Download one level at a time, and have her complete three puzzles a week. Even though the exercises require brain work, they feel like fun.

7. Play at least one thinking game every weekend with the entire family.

Use the protected weekend together for some fun family game time that improves her thinking skills. With a competitive brother and dad, she is sure to enjoy the challenge of beating them! Old favorite board games like chess, Chinese checkers, *Clue*, *Monopoly*, or backgammon will work. If you want to add to your collection, look for games that require her to develop a strategy. Historical board games like *Oregon* have players assume an identity and play out a piece of American history in 1846. In this particular game, players pretend they are pioneers as they plan how to cultivate the land and build the infrastructure of community.

For times when she would rather be alone, she can play any number of *Nancy Drew* mystery games on her computer.

8. Teach her the fundamental elements of literature.

Literary analysis does not have to be that difficult, and you don't need to purchase a thirty-six week literature curriculum to teach literary criticism. All you have to do is think like a writer, and since she is already working on her own mystery novel, it is time to give her all the tools that she needs to create her own masterpiece. You are also an avid fan of narrative prose, so the first step in teaching her the fundamentals of literary analysis is refreshing your own knowledge of the tools. First, find one comprehensive "how to" book for adults under the Library of Congress book classification category entitled "literary criticism." Three of my favorite resources for thinking like a writer are:

- *Reading Between the Lines*, Gene Edward Veith
- *How to Read Literature Like a Professor*, Thomas Foster
- *The Reader over your Shoulder*, Ralph Graves and Alan Hodge

Once you have read at least one of these books, you can decide what concepts to teach in the context of her ongoing literature selections and prose compositions. When she is a few years older, you can let her read the same book that you read on literary criticism to fulfill part of her English credit.

9. Require "one-idea" paragraphs when she writes.

Marie's compositions are written in a conversational tone which means they read more like a stream of consciousness than several units of thought intentionally placed in a certain order. She occasionally indents her essay, but the beginning sentence of each new paragraph does not necessarily introduce a new topic. Teach her how to write a simple one-idea paragraph with a topic sentence and three to seven supporting sentences.

Every sentence should relate back to the first sentence of the paragraph, or it should not be in the paragraph.

Obviously, she has a lot of ideas to communicate, so it might help her to organize her thoughts before she begins the essay by creating an outline. An outline is like a road map that takes the writer to the final destination. In her essay on the Janette Oke book, she could have structured the paper in several ways: chronological paragraphs, thematic paragraphs, or character paragraphs. In a few years when has mastered the one-idea paragraph, you can introduce her to the great variety of paragraphs by getting a copy of *A Writer's Guide to Powerful Paragraphs* by Victor Pellegrino which demonstrates how to structure information in thirty different ways. Most people would never need this level of expertise, but since she is interested in pursuing a writing career, depth of knowledge is necessary to refine her craft.

10. Encourage her to perfect the interpretive speech.

Drama is a favorite extracurricular activity as evidenced by her eager participation in several plays, musicals, and camps. Interpretive speeches are like acting without costumes or props. One speaker assumes multiple characters by adopting various voices and personalities to interpret a piece of literature. There are four possible types of interpretive speech: dramatic, humorous, duo, and open.

Since her tastes in movies and books leans toward the serious historical novel or mystery, help her find an appropriate selection from literature so that she can perfect the dramatic speech. Jane Austen, Nancy Drew, and Trixie Belden fiction would be a good starting point since she is already so familiar with the stories. As she reads, she is already interpreting the meaning of the content in her mind, so taking it one step further and acting out the content should be relatively easy for her. Instead of editing an entire narrative, select one chapter to cut to a ten minute length.

Marie's Weekly Plan

- Use the spell check tool every time you write an essay

- Work pre-algebra lessons (weekly)

- Draw and label observations while on weekly nature walks

- Develop and execute a garden plot on your property

- Read selected biographies or autobiographies (weekly)
- Work three *Mindbenders* puzzles a week
- Play at least one game with your family on the weekend
- Learn the elements of literature
- Draft an outline every time you write
- Perfect the one-idea paragraph
- Memorize and deliver an interpretive speech

Progress Report

Sometime around the end of the semester, take an inventory with Marie of her progress. Ask her what she has and has not enjoyed about the past few weeks. If there were steps that did not work for Marie, eliminate them from the next semester and come up with an alternative plan.

Pull all of her work and take a big picture look at whether her skills have improved especially in solving logic puzzles, recording her nature observations, and consistently writing a one-idea paragraph. Keep working on those areas that need improvement.

Chapter 58
Action Steps for Mark and Julia

Marie's action steps are segregated below into (a) one-time tasks like purchase books and (b) recurring tasks like weekly reading. Once Mark and Julia have thought about the suggested plan, they can decide what ideas they will implement and allocate the work amongst themselves. There are certain teaching goals that Mark is best equipped to handle while other teaching goals are clearly in Julia's domain.

Preliminary ONE-TIME Action Steps

- ❏ Purchase a sketchbook and colored pencils
- ❏ Purchase garden materials for her project
- ❏ Purchase a biography or autobiography reference guide
- ❏ Purchase *Mindbenders* software
- ❏ Purchase a resource for learning literary elements
- ❏ Help her select a piece of literature to interpret

* * * * *

RECURRING Action Steps

- Proofread her written compositions to make sure she is using the spell check tool
- Send her outside once a week to document her nature observations
- Play one game a weekend with her
- Teach her a new literary element periodically
- Teach her how to write a one idea paragraph

Appendices

&

Assessment Tools

INTERVIEW QUESTIONS

About you:

1. What are your strengths? Weaknesses?
2. What are your favorite pastimes?
3. What special gifts do you have?
4. Have you ever attended public school? If so, for how long?
5. Was school a good or bad experience?
6. What are your favorite memories about school? Least favorite?
7. Do you have an undergraduate or graduate degree? In what area?
8. Did you have a career before you began home schooling?
9. What other events or experiences do you bring to parenting?
10. Are you committed to many activities outside the home?

About your spouse:

1. What are his strengths? Weaknesses?
2. What are his favorite pastimes?
3. What special gifts does he have?
4. Did he ever attend public school? If so, for how long?
5. Was school a good or bad experience?
6. What are his favorite memories about school? Least favorite?
7. Does he have an undergraduate or graduate degree? In what area?
8. What is his career? How long is his typical work day?
9. Does he participate in home schooling?
10. What other events or experiences does he bring to parenting?

About each child:

1. What are his strengths? Weaknesses?
2. What are his favorite pastimes and interests?
3. What special gifts or talents does he have?
4. Does he play an instrument or participate in an athletic activity?
5. Did he ever attend public school? If so, for how long? Was it a good experience?
6. What does he most like about home school? Dislike?
7. Are there any developmental issues that might impact how you teach?
8. What kind of books does he enjoy?
9. What is his favorite subject?

10. If you had to choose adjectives to describe him, what would they be?

About home schooling content:

1. What were the first products that you bought for your home school?
2. Did you use a particular brand of curriculum?
3. Were you happy with the results achieved from these products?
4. Briefly describe the resources you are using for teaching:

   a. religion
   b. literature
   c. history
   d. composition
   e. grammar
   f. math
   g. science
   h. other

5. Do you ever feel like you're trying to do too much? Too little?
6. Are there other things that you want to teach that you haven't had time to do yet?
7. What general areas do you feel qualified to teach?
8. Are there any areas of study in which you feel inadequate?
9. Do you need a refresher course in any areas?
10. Do you have the time to study or would you rather have someone help you?

About home schooling philosophy:

1. When were you first introduced to the idea of home schooling?
2. Why did you decide to teach your kids at home?
3. How long have you been home schooling?
4. What moments related to home schooling have brought you the greatest joy?
5. What moments have brought you the most frustration?
6. How organized would you say your home school is?
7. How structured is your typical day?
8. Do you take breaks throughout the calendar year?
9. Do you follow the public school calendar?
10. Do you have a dedicated room just for school?

11. If you could pick one obstacle to feeling good about your teaching, what would it be?
12. What is your biggest concern about giving your kids a classical education?

SHORT VOWELS

a	e	i	o	u
cat	jet	sip	pop	cub
mat	net	zip	cot	mug
rat	wet	rip	pot	bug
hat	red	did	mom	bud
ham	bed	kit	hop	hug
man	leg	sit	rod	run
pan	men	lid	mop	gum
cab	pen	dig	hot	tub
ax	ten	pig	dot	sun

LONG VOWELS

a-e	ai	ay	ee	ea
tape	nail	hay	jeep	leaf
pane	pail	gray	feet	sea
cape	train	tray	bee	pea
mane	rain	pray	tree	feat
vane	braid	spray	sleep	heat
cane	maid	bay	jeep	peat

ey	y	ie	i-e	y
key	fifty	chief	hide	sky
monkey	bunny	shield	wipe	cry
money	funny	priest	twine	dry
honey	sneezy	thief	stripe	fry
donkey	sleepy	grief	dime	try

igh	o-e	oa	ow	u-e
night	rope	goat	row	cube
light	home	soap	crow	tube
thigh	bone	coal	bowl	tune
fight	robe	coat	mow	cute
sight	smoke	foam	snow	mule

CONSONANTS

Sound	Example
p	pen, spin, tip
b	but, web
t	two, sting, bet
d	do, odd
ch	chair, nature, teach
g	ginger, joy, edge
k	cat, kill, skin, queen, unique, thick
g	go, get, beg
f	fool, enough, leaf, off, photo
v	voice, have
thh	thing, teeth
th	this, breathe, father
s	see, city, pass
z	zoo, rose
sh	she, sure, emotion, leash
jz	pleasure, beige, seizure
x	Scottish loch
h	ham
m	man, ham
n	no, tin
ng	ringer, sing, finger, drink
l	left, bell
r	run, very
kw	queen
yh	yes
wh	what

CONSONANT BLENDS

cl	nd	nt	sl	st
clan	hand	ant	slip	stop
club	sand	tent	slot	stem
clap	pond	dent	sled	step
clip	wind	bunt	slug	cast
clam	bind	burnt	sleep	last

* * * * *

CONSONANT DIGRAPHS

ch	ck	kn	ll	mb	ng
chin	duck	knob	will	lamb	fang
chip	black	knot	well	jamb	swing
chop	clock	knit	bell	comb	ring
bench	trick	knife	spill	thumb	string
lunch	pick	know	tell	limb	lung

nk	qu	sh	tch	th	wr
pink	quilt	ship	watch	thick	wrap
tank	quit	shield	catch	thin	wrench
think	squid	shot	patch	thump	wring
drink	quack	sash	switch	path	wrist
blink	quick	dish	pitch	bath	wren

PHONETIC ROOTS

Root		Root		Root		Root		Root	
-ab	cab	-e	me	-ice	mice	-o	no	-op	mop
-ack	tack	-ea	sea	-id	lid	-oad	toad	-ope	rope
-ad	sad	-eak	beak	-ide	ride	-oak	oak	-ot	pot
-ade	made	-eal	seal	-ie	pie	-oat	goat	-ound	round
-ag	bag	-ean	bean	-ig	pig	-ob	bob	-out	shout
-age	page	-ear	ear	-ight	light	-ock	lock	-ow	cow
-ail	nail	-eat	eat	-ike	bike	-od	rod	-ow	crow
-ain	train	-ed	bed	-ill	hill	-og	dog	-own	clown
-ait	wait	-ee	bee	-im	him	-oice	voice	-oy	toy
-ake	cake	-eed	seed	-ime	time	-oil	boil		
-all	ball	-eel	wheel	-in	pin	-oin	coin	-ub	sub
-ale	whale	-een	green	-ine	nine	-oke	joke	-uck	duck
-am	ham	-eep	jeep	-ing	ring	-old	gold	-ug	rug
-ame	name	-eet	feet	-ink	pink	-ole	mole	-um	gum
-an	pan	-ell	bell	-tion	action	-oll	roll	-un	sun
-and	sand	-en	ten	-ip	ship	-one	bone	-ture	future
-ap	map	-end	send	-ish	fish	-ong	song	-us	bus
-at	cat	-ent	went	-it	hit	-ook	book	-ut	nut
-ate	gate	-et	net	-ite	kite	-ool	school		
-aw	saw			-ive	five	-oom	broom	-y	cry
-ay	hay			-ive	give	-oon	moon	-y	sunny

SIGHT WORDS – 1

a	can	her	many	see	us
about	come	here	me	she	very
after	day	him	much	so	was
again	did	his	my	some	we
all	do	how	new	take	were
an	down	I	no	that	what
and	eat	if	not	the	when
any	for	in	of	their	which
are	from	is	old	them	who
as	get	it	on	then	will
at	give	just	one	there	with
be	go	know	or	they	work
been	good	like	other	this	would
before	had	little	our	three	you
boy	has	long	out	to	your
but	have	make	put	two	
by	he	man	up		

SIGHT WORDS – 2

also	color	home	must	red	think
am	could	house	name	right	too
another	dear	into	near	run	tree
away	each	kind	never	saw	under
back	ear	last	next	say	until
ball	end	leave	night	school	upon
because	far	left	only	seem	use
best	find	let	open	shall	want
better	first	live	over	should	way
big	five	look	own	soon	where
black	found	made	people	stand	while
book	four	may	play	such	white
both	friend	men	please	sure	wish
box	girl	more	present	tell	why
bring	got	morning	pretty	than	year
call	hand	most	ran	these	
came	high	mother	read	thing	

SIGHT WORDS – 3

along	didn't	food	keep	sat	though
always	does	full	letter	second	today
anything	dog	funny	longer	set	took
around	don't	gave	love	seven	town
ask	door	goes	might	show	try
ate	dress	green	money	sing	turn
bed	early	grow	myself	sister	walk
brown	eight	hat	now	sit	warm
buy	every	happy	o'clock	six	wash
car	eyes	hard	off	sleep	water
carry	face	head	once	small	woman
clean	fall	hear	order	start	write
close	fast	help	pair	stop	yellow
clothes	fat	hold	part	ten	yes
coat	fine	hope	ride	thank	yesterday
cold	fire	hot	round	third	
cut	fly	jump	same	those	

READING EXCERPT – 1

Then we saw him pick up
All the things that were down.
He picked up the cake,
And the rake, and the gown,
And the milk, and the strings,
And the books, and the dish.
And the fan, and the cup,
And the ship, and the fish.
And he put them away.
Then he said, "That is that."
And then he was gone
With a tip of his hat.

(Taken from *The Cat in the Hat* by Dr. Seuss)

READING EXCERPT – 2

"Good-bye, Little Bird," said Sister Bear. "Fly away and be happy." On her finger was the sparrow that the Bear family had taken in because it had an injured leg. Papa Bear had made a splint for it out of a toothpick and strips of tape.

Brother and Sister had named it Tweetie and had taken care of it for about a week. But now it was time to remove the splint and let the bird go back to nature, where it belonged. It hopped onto a twig, then took wing.

(Taken from *The Berenstain Bears' Trouble with Pets*, Stan & Jan Berenstain)

READING EXCERPT – 3

There was a loud rumbling sound, as of stones rolling and falling, and suddenly light streamed in, real light, the plain light of day. A low door-like opening appeared at the end of the chamber beyond Frodo's feet; and there was Tom's head (hat, feather, and all) framed against the light of the sun rising red behind him. The light fell upon the floor, and upon the faces of the three hobbits lying beside Frodo. They did not stir, but the sickly hue had left them. They looked now as if they were only very deeply asleep.

(Taken from *The Fellowship of the Ring*, J.R.R. Tolkien)

READING EXCERPT – 4

A curious thrush perching in a gnarled pear tree watched the two figures make their way at a sedate pace in the direction of Great Hall, one clad in the dark greeny-brown of the order, the other garbed in the lighter green of a novice. They conversed earnestly in low tones. Thinking what a clever bird he was, the thrush swooped down on the basket that had been left behind. Twisters! The basket contained only hard nuts, locked tight within their shells. Feining lack of interest, lest any other birds had been witness to his silly mistake, he began whistling jauntily a few bars of his melodious summer song, strolling nonchalantly over to the cloister walls in search of snails.

(Taken from *Redwall*, Brian Jacques)

READING EXCERPT – 5

Now though, if you wish me to fight it out and do battle,

make the rest of the Trojans sit down, and all the Achaians,

and set me in the middle with Menelaos the warlike

to fight together for the sake of Helen and all her possessions.

That one of us who wins and is proved stronger, let him

take the possessions fairly and the woman, and lead her homeward.

But the rest of you, having cut your oaths of faith and friendship,

dwell, you in Troy where the soil is rich, while those others return

home to horse pasturing Argos, and Achaia the land of fair women.

(Taken from *The Iliad*, Homer, book three, v.67-74)

COMMON SPELLING RULES

Comparative: adjective + **er** (quick to quick**er**)

Superlative: adjective + **est** (quick to quick**est**)

Past tense: verb + **ed** (turn to turn**ed**)

Gerunds or Present Participles: verb + **ing** (turn to turn**ing**)

Adverb: adjective + **ly** (sweet to sweet**ly**)

Plural: noun + **s** (boy to boys)
                                      verb + **s** (run to runs)

-ie or –ei: -i before –e except after –c

Don't forget that in English there are always **exceptions** to the rules!

Examples:

Superlative: if the adjective ends in –y, drop
                        the –y and add an –i (happy to
                        happ**i**est)

-ie or –ei: if the sound is a long "a," spell –ei
                        (n**ei**ghbor, w**ei**gh, sl**ei**gh)

PARTS OF SPEECH

Noun
Verb
Adjective
Adverb
Pronoun
Preposition
Interjection
Conjunction

SENTENCE STRUCTURE

Types (declarative, interrogative, imperative, exclamatory)
Kinds (simple, compound, complex, compound-complex)

Subject (noun clauses)
Predicate (verb, direct & indirect objects, predicate nominative & adjective)
Modifiers (adjectives, possessive nouns, appositive, adverbs)
Verbals (participles, gerunds, infinitives)

GRAMMAR PROPERTIES

Of nouns:

Types (common, proper)
Number (singular, plural)
Gender (male, female)
Case (nominative, objective, possessive)
Declension

Of verbs:

Principal parts (infinitive, present, past, present participle, past participle)
Conjugation (progressive, emphatic)
Voice (active, passive)
Mood (indicative, imperative, subjunctive)
Placement (transitive, intransitive)
Agreement of Subject and Verb

Of pronouns:

Kinds (personal, interrogative, demonstrative, indefinite, reflexive)
Agreement of pronoun, noun, and verb

Of modifiers:

Forms (comparative, superlative)
Dangling
Misplaced

PREPOSITIONS

aboard	at	despite	of	to
about	before	down	off	towards
above	behind	during	on	under
across	below	except	outside	underneath
after	beneath	for	over	until
against	beside(s)	from	past	unto
along	between	in	regarding	up
amid	beyond	inside	since	upon
among	but	into	through	with
around	by	near	throughout	within
			'til	without

PREPOSITIONAL PHRASES

according to...
because of...
by way of...
in addition to...
in front of...
in place of...
in regard to...
in spite of...
instead of...
on account of...
out of...

STANDARD CONJUNCTIONS

and	if	or	but	so
both	for	also	else	further
	likewise	whether	otherwise	
		as well as		

Not only...but also

whether...or

either...or

neither...or

SUBORDINATING CONJUNCTIONS
(used in adverb clauses)

after	as though	in order that	though	whereas
although	because	lest	unless	wherever
as	before	since	until	while
as if	but that	so that	when	why
as long as	how	than	whenever	
as soon as	if	that	where	

PUNCTUATION

Capital letters
Period
Question Mark
Exclamation Point
Comma
Semicolon
Colon
Italics
Underlining
Quotation Marks
Dash
Hyphen
Parentheses
Brackets
Ellipsis

SEQUENCES

What patterns do you see in each line?
What are the next 3 numbers?

2   4   6   8   10

5   10   15   20   25   30

275   250   225   200   175

1   1   2   3   5   8   13   21

11   121   1331   14641


```
                1
              1   1
            1   2   1
          1   3   3   1
        1   4   6   4   1
      1   5   10   10   5   1
    1   6   15   20   15   6   1
  1   7   21   35   35   21   7   1
1   8   28   56   70   56   28   8   1
1   9   36 84   126   126 84   36   9   1
1  10   45 120 210   252 210 120 45   10   1
```

NUMBER SQUARES

Look at the pattern of shading. Are the shaded numbers even or odd? Will the squares lettered A, B, C, and D be shaded?

1	2	3	4	5	6	7	8	9	10
11	12	13	14	15	16	17	18	19	20
21	22	23	24	25	26	27	28	29	30
31	32	33	34	35	36	37	38	39	40
41	42	43							
			A						
					B				
									C
		D							100

Look at the pattern of shading. Are the shaded numbers even or odd? Will the squares lettered A, B, C, and D be shaded?

1	2	3	4	5	6	7	8	9	10
11	12	13	14	15	16	17	18	19	20
21	22	23	24	25	26	27	28	29	30
		A		B			C		
					D				100

INDUCTION

Move from the specific to the general like this:

Identify the particular. (A poppy)
Identify the characteristics. (Red)
Conclude for the general. (**All** poppies are red)

Example:

I found a red poppy in the meadow; so, all poppies must be red.

Now it's your turn to conclude on the facts:

"The fountain at the park" is "outside," therefore _____.
Is your conclusion true or false?

Particular (specific)	Characteristics	Conclusion (general)	T/F
the fountain at the park	outside		
a poodle being walked	pink collar and leash		
the grass in my yard	green		
my favorite stuffed animal	teddy bear		
the capital letter A	shaped like a triangle		
a Christmas wreath	green holly and red berries		
the tiger at the zoo	orange and black stripes		
the tomato on Veggie Tales	named Bob		
a McD's hamburger	shaped like a circle		

DEDUCTION

Move from the general to the specific like this:

Identify the class. (Wasps)
Identify the characteristics. (Stingers)
Think of a specific example. (**That** one will bite)

Example:

Be careful of **that big** wasp. **It** might sting you!

Now it's your turn to conclude on the facts.

"Triangles," have "three sides," therefore _____.
Is your conclusion true or false?

Class (general)	Characteristics	Conclusion (specific)	T/F
triangles	three sides		
baseball games	nine innings		
evergreen trees	leaves stay on in winter		
birds	fly south in winter		
paper	sharp edges		
dogs	chew on bones		
cars	carry passengers		
holidays	celebrate and play		
desserts	taste sweet		

ANALOGIES

Analogies are used to draw comparisons like this:

hand (is to) palm (as) foot (is to) arch
hand : palm :: foot : arch

* * * * *

Now you try it.

cat : meow :: dog : _____

rope : thick :: string : _____

car : vehicle :: yo-yo : _____

loose : tight :: east : _____

spring : season :: August : _____

sheep : lamb :: bear : _____

milk : drink :: cake : _____

horse : hooves :: dog : _____

library : books :: bank : _____

CONFIRMATION AND REFUTATION

Confirm the argument:

Explain the issue.
Point out the merits of the argument.
Give examples that support your position.
Prove that position is probable, consistent, proper, or reasonable

Refute the argument:

Explain the issue.
Point out the problems with the argument.
Give examples that support your position.
Prove that position is improbable, inconsistent, improper, or unreasonable.

Confirm and refute the following five arguments:

"Early to bed...early to rise...makes a man healthy, wealthy, and wise."
(Franklin)

George Washington couldn't tell a lie.

Paul Bunyan had a blue ox named Babe.

Why opossums have bare tails.

"Humor is mankind's greatest blessing." (Twain)

LITERARY ELEMENTS

These essential elements of a story constitute the structure of the literature. Every good story has all or most of these elements. The author intentionally puts these parts together to form a unified whole much like the systems of a car all work together to create a whole operational vehicle.

Plot
Characters
Point of View
Conflict
Foreshadowing
Irony
Tone or mood
Symbolism
Theme
Imagery
Figurative Language

PLOT

- Exposition - establishes the setting, introduces the characters, creates the tone, and provides other facts necessary to understanding

- Foreshadowing - hints or clues that suggest what will happen later

- Inciting Force - the event or character that triggers the conflict

- Conflict – four forces that oppose man (another man, nature, society, or self)

- Rising Action - a series of events that begins with the inciting force and ends with the climax

- Crisis - the conflict reaches an intense turning point as the opposing forces meet; usually occurs before or at the same time as the climax

- Climax – the result of the crisis at which the outcome of the conflict can be predicted; the moment of highest emotion

- Falling Action – also called denouement, these post-climatic events wrap up the loose ends of the story

- Resolution – concludes the action

CHARACTERS

- Major
  - Protagonist – hero
  - Antagonist – opposes hero
  - Foil – provides a contrast to the hero
  - Qualities of major characters
    - i. 3D – well-rounded person with good and bad points
    - ii. Dynamic - they change inside and outside during course of story

- Minor
  - Qualities
    - i. 2D – have 1-2 interesting characteristics; not balanced
    - ii. Static – flat in that they do not change during the story

CREATIVE WRITING

Personal narratives
Journals
Letters
Short stories
Scripts
Lyrics
Poems
Novels

EXPOSITORY WRITING

Mini reports
Essays
Research papers
Journalism articles
Interviews
Blog posts
Testimony
Book reports
Critiques
Arguments
Technical writing

THE FIVE PARAGRAPH ESSAY FORMAT

Hook: Grab attention

Quote, statistic, or story
"Robin Hood and Little John are walking through the forest…"

Introduction: Paragraph 1

Thesis
The legend of Robin Hood has been shaped by word of mouth stories, later writings, and recent movies.

Body: Paragraph 2

Supporting detail 1
For over a thousand years, grandparents have been sharing the many legends of Robin Hood with their grandchildren at bedtime.

Body: Paragraph 3

Supporting detail 2
Once the printing press was invented, these oral legends of Robin and his merry men were transferred to the written word.

Body: Paragraph 4

Supporting detail 3
More recently, movie studios like Walt Disney and Miramax have continued to retell the stories of Robin to young viewers.

Conclusion: Paragraph 5

Restate thesis and echo hook
Animated cartoons, books, and bedtime stories have all served to perpetuate the legend of Robin Hood.

"Robin Hood and Little John were walking through the forest…"

DRESS UPS*

Technique	Example
adverb (called the **-ly** word)	repeated**ly**
strong verb	violate
quality adjective	horrendous
who/which	the boy **who** came to dinner the 2nd course **which** was yummy
because	I want to serve **because** it is right to do so.
www.asia	**when** the moon comes out **while** the laundry is drying **where** a little frog jumps **as** we go to Granny's house **since** they all departed **if** I could change the world **although** nothing can be done

*See *Institute for Excellence in Writing* for full details.

SENTENCE OPENERS*

Technique	Example
subject	**Elephants** use their trunks for drinking.
prepositional	**Between** the slices of bread
-ly	**Excitedly,** the young child opened the
-ing	**Screaming** with delight, she unwrapped
clausal (www.asia)	**When we were young,** we played jacks. **While I was walking,** a little bird **Where I used to live,** the summers were **As if that wasn't enough,** she surprised **Since we were all alone,** I decided to **If I were you,** I would learn how to **Although it was late,** the kids watched
very short sentence	Jesus wept.
-ed	**Frustrated,** the shop owner drew the
transitional	**Nevertheless,** the jackrabbit scurried

*See *Institute for Excellence in Writing* for full details.

DECORATIONS*

Technique	Example
question	Do you believe in fairies?
conversation	He said, **"Of course, I do!"**
3 short staccato sentences	Bells pealed. Birds chirped. Bees stung.
dramatic opening	Owls screeched as the trees shivered.
dramatic closing	Never again would the two meet.
simile	smells **like fresh summer rain**
metaphor	a house cat **is a monster** when it comes to
alliteration	**smelly, stinky, slimy** sludge
assonance	c**a**t in the h**a**t s**a**t next to the b**a**t

*See *Institute for Excellence in Writing* for full details.

TRIPLES*

Technique	Example
Preposition repetition	**from** me-**from** you-**from** them
Clausal repetition	**combing her hair** (3 times)
Repeating –ing	sing**ing**, danc**ing**, and laugh**ing**
Repeating –ly	soft**ly**, tender**ly**, and calm**ly**
Repeating noun	fragile **glass**-empty **glass**-broken **glass**
Repeating verb	llamas **spit**-camels **spit**-little boys **spit**
Repeating adjective	**soft** blanket-**soft** pillow-**soft** slippers

*See *Institute for Excellence in Writing* for full details.

ADVANCED DRESS UPS*

Technique	Example
dual adjectives	**sleek, shiny** motorcycle
dual adverbs	lion **stealthily** crept and **fiercely** roared
dual verbs	dolphin **plunged** and **leapt**
noun clause	the man**, in his ranger clothes,** hurried
adjectival teeter-totter	the **difficult yet enjoyable** task
adverbial teeter-totter	**substantially and predictably** completed

*See *Institute for Excellence in Writing* for full details.

ESSAY VERB PROMPTS

These verbs are often included in the SAT essay prompts. Each verb requires a certain response.

If *your verb is:*	*Do this:*
Analyze	Take it apart to see how each part works
Compare	Point out likenesses between things
Contrast	Point out differences between things
Define	Answer the question "what is it?" by first classifying it; then discuss the specific features that make it different from other members of the same class.
Describe	Give a word picture
Discuss	Examine in detail
Evaluate	Determine if the author's purpose has been achieved by applying standards of judgment; include evidence from the work
Explain	Give reasons for something being the way it is; how or why with examples from the text
Illustrate, demonstrate	Provide examples to support a point
Interpret	Give the meaning or significance

* * * * *

Here are some example topic sentences using these verb prompts:

Analyze the legend of Robin Hood.

> The legend of Robin Hood has been shaped by word of mouth stories, later writings, and recent movies.

Compare Reepicheep and Truffle.

> Reepicheep and Truffle share many similarities in body and spirit.

Contrast Martin the Warrior and Lord Urthstripe.

> Martin the Warrior and Lord Urthstripe are vastly different characters in size and loyalty.

Define personification.

> Personification is a figure of speech that gives human qualities to nonhuman things like the whomping willow in *Chamber of Secrets*.

Describe the setting of Hannibal's Alps.

> When Hannibal's army crossed over the Alps, the wind was frigid and blustery making the journey treacherously dangerous.

Discuss the fellowship that delivered the ring to Mordor.

> The fellowship that delivered the ring to Mordor was comprised of men, elves, dwarves, and hobbits.

Evaluate the effectiveness of Tolkien's use of grotesque details to describe the Orcs.

> Tolkien was extremely effective in using grotesque details like rotted teeth, raspy voices, and angry violence to reveal the Orcs.

Explain Frodo's sadness when he had to leave on the ship at the end of the movie.

> Frodo's sadness in departure on the ship relates to deep friendships and the sorrow that leaving his friends brings.

Illustrate Aslan as a Christ like figure.

Aslan is a Christ like figure because he gives his own life on the table in place of Edmund.

Interpret the significance of red hair in Anne of Green Gables.

Anne's red hair is extremely significant because it symbolizes her feisty, spontaneous temperament.

About the Author

&

After practicing nine years as a CPA with Price Waterhouse and Clopay Corporation, Diane Binkley Lockman cheerfully surrendered her career so that she could stay home with Meredith and Connor until they went to school. When Meredith was in first grade, Diane heard about home schooling and started reading all that she could about this alternative to public education. Within weeks, Diane persuaded David to let her pull the kids out of school and start teaching them at home. Partners in teaching, Diane and David are now giving their children the classical Christian education that they never received in the public school system.

Convinced that more parents would give their children an authentic classical home education if they only knew how, Diane launched *The Classical Scholar* (http://classicalscholar.com) in 2006. An online teaching resource for home school parents, *The Classical Scholar* offers practical articles, videos, podcasts, and teleconferences that demonstrate exactly how to execute an authentic classical education in the home. With the aid of these resources, homeschool parents can easily take what they have learned from Diane and strategically create a customized curriculum that uniquely meet the needs of each child. Diane also teaches live classes to home school teens in her community and speaks at state and local home school conventions.

When she's not reading, writing, managing the kids' education, or teaching live classes, Diane enjoys sewing period costumes like her recent *My Fair Lady* and *Lord of the Rings* designs.